TESTIMONIALS

Reader Responses

Marian uses her captivating sense of humor, her all-too-familiar life experiences, and her thorough knowledge of the Bible to create an engaging, relatable book daring the reader to stop living in a dead-end world and to start living the adventure-filled life God has in store for us. Due to the personal and relatable nature of this book, including priceless references to *Sex and the City*, the reader's mind, body, and soul become a part of the stories and circumstances. Marian provides a strong platform for leading readers from what we think is a fulfilling life to one where we hand control over to the endless opportunities the Lord has in store for us.

— *Julie (Houston, Texas)*

After reading Marian Jordan's engaging book, you will only regret you didn't read it years ago! You will laugh. You will cry. You will pass it on to a friend.   — *Toni (Houston)*

Audience Responses to *Sex and the City Uncovered* Talks

Sex and the City Uncovered really hit home, as I'm sure it did for most of the women. I am without a doubt a "Samantha" and am at the point that I just can't take it anymore. Living this way isn't worth it.   — *Jessica, age 25*

Sex and the City Uncovered was pivotal in my walk as a Christian. Upon hearing Marian's message, for the first time

I was able to hear my story in another woman's life. She made me feel like I was not alone. After years of depression and looking for the world to fill my emptiness, I found myself seeking the Lord. There is such a need for women to hear their pain and struggles reflected by godly women, and I experienced that through the *Sex and the City* series. Marian taught me that there is hope in Christ.

— *Shannon, age 34*

Thank you for the awesome "girl talk." I was truly moved and enlightened by your message. It's refreshing to listen to someone who is so raw and honest when they speak. I can absolutely relate to the things you were telling us.

— *Kara, age 27*

I had been visiting Second Baptist Church only a month prior to attending the *Sex & the City, Uncovered* event. I knew only a few acquaintances and was quite nervous to even walk in the door. I'm a shy individual to begin with, but I was bound and determined to meet people and make friends, so I reasoned this was a perfect way to do it. As I parked my car and walked through the door, I remember thinking to myself, *What am I doing here, and will I really fit in with these girls?*

As the lights lowered to signal the beginning of the show, I sat back and again wondered why I was here. Marian Jordan came on the stage, and I sat there and listened while what she was saying tugged at my heart. Her message was loud and clear to me: there is more to this life.

More than boys, fashionable clothes, fancy cars, and good friends. I sat there soaking in all that was said and knew I'd been missing "it" all my life. The "it" was Jesus Christ, my Savior and Redeemer. I had been missing Him for twenty-five years and absolutely refused to live anymore without Him. As Marian wrapped up, I felt at peace in knowing that I was meant to be in that very seat surrounded by hundreds of women, many of whom may have come to the very realization that all we need in this life is Jesus Christ. I felt the very presence of God in that room that night, and it was overwhelming.

It's been almost two years since I stepped outside that theater, and my life has taken a totally different avenue. Being a follower of Jesus Christ has been amazing. It's not always easy, but the joy in my heart is overflowing. I know for a fact that many women's lives were affected that night by Marian's message. Some of those women have become my best friends, and it's amazing to see their walk with the Lord grow every day . . . as does mine.   — *Stacia, age 27*

Marian Jordan's insight and teaching during the *Sex & the City Uncovered* series triggered a major transformation in my life. I remember how much her stories of failed attempts to find fulfillment in empty relationships, professional pursuits, and sheer consumerism deeply resonated with my own sad experiences. I admired the courage she had to tell the ugly truth and the triumphant victory that God effected in her life. It gave me hope.   — *Dalia, age 35*

sex and the city
UNCOVERED

EXPOSING THE EMPTINESS AND HEALING THE HURT

marian jordan

B&H
PUBLISHING GROUP
Nashville, Tennessee

ISBN: 978-0-8054-4669-2

Published by B & H Publishing Group,
Nashville, Tennessee

Dewey Decimal Classification: 248.843
Subject Heading: WOMEN \ CHRISTIAN LIFE
CONDUCT OF LIFE

This B&H book is not affiliated or connected with, nor sponsored, endorsed, or necessarily approved by, HBO or the *Sex and the City* television program or book.

Unless otherwise designated, Scripture quotations are from the Holman Christian Standard Bible, copyright © 1999, 2000, 2002, 2003 by Holman Bible Publishers, Nashville, Tennessee; all rights reserved. Other Bible translations quoted are noted as MSG, *The Message,* copyright © 1993, 1994, 1995, 1996, 2000, 2001, 2002 by Eugene H. Peterson; NASB, copyright © 1960, 1962, 1963, 1968, 1971, 1972, 1973, 1975, 1977, 1995 by The Lockman Foundation; NIV, New International Version, copyright © 1973, 1978, 1984 by International Bible Society; and NLT, New Living Translation, copyright © 1996, 2004 by Tyndale Charitable Trust, used by permission of Tyndale House Publishers.

11 10 09 08 07   1 2 3 4 5 6 7 8 9 10 11 12 13 14 15

Contents

This book is dedicated to every girl who is looking for love.

The
Sex and the City
Life

I still haven't found what I'm looking for.
BONO OF U2

I knew he was trouble the moment I saw him. *Big trouble.* We first met standing in line at a bar in our college town. I'm sure I had a fake ID and was rehearsing my speech for the bouncer when I spotted him in the crowd of hammered college students. He oozed unattainable. I-had-to-have-him!

Young and dizzy with independence, I was nineteen years old the fall semester of my freshman year. Some say the freshman year is a rite of passage: 8:00 a.m. classes, keg parties, sorority rush, and potluck roommate debacles—simply a cesspool of bad choices. What's funny to me now is that I thought I was so mature; I guess my newfound freedom went to my head like an ICEE headache on a hot summer day.

Girls, I'm not gonna lie—he was hot. I can just see him now, wearing khakis, a polo, and a devilish grin. He made my knees weak when our eyes met. I was sold. After a few weeks of flirting at fraternity parties over stale beer and Jell-O shots, we progressed to a *"real"* relationship—at least as close as you ever get in college. Yes, ladies, we were officially "hanging out." But in the land of undecided majors and even more uncertain futures, I had no certainty that he was going to be around for very long.

I'll give it to you straight: I really wanted this guy to like me. No, I take that back; it was more than that. I wanted it all. I wanted him to *l-o-v-e* me—the kind of love that banishes insecurities and makes a girl feel . . . adored. Not that I was looking for my M.R.S. degree, but I was for sure looking for the security that comes from being a couple. So, I needed to do something, and I needed to act quickly. It's not as if I was the only new girl on campus. Either trash-can punch or hormones kill brain cells because I thought that going with him back to his place late one night was the answer. Boy, was I wrong.

Frankly, it was nothing like the movies. It wasn't fun or romantic; actually, it was quite awkward. But in my naïve young mind I truly believed I would find what I was looking for in this guy's dorm room. What was it that I was looking for? Reflecting on it, I honestly think

I believed he would love me if I finally gave in. I know it is so cliché, a girl having sex in hopes of finding love. I did and he didn't. The relationship didn't even last as long as football season; and the truth of the matter is, I didn't find what I was looking for that night in his dorm room. Instead, I found a doorway into a lifestyle that would bring me tears, regrets, and emptiness. Like Bono, I still hadn't found what I was looking for.

My story isn't all too different from other girls my age. I grew up singing Madonna's lyrics and taking my dating cues from *Saved by the Bell* and *90210*. As a young girl I had ideals of purity and desired to wait until marriage to have sex. But something happened. Was it temptation, a desire for acceptance, or simply the need to feel loved? Or perhaps I was more influenced by my culture than I realized. Whatever the case may be, I left the moral upbringing of my childhood and plunged into a world that said, "Just do it."

More than a decade has passed since that night but in many ways a lifetime. While unremarkable in some respects, that night was a defining moment for the rest of my story. The consequences of that decision shaped and formed the girl I would become for the next few years.

As a result of that decision, I quickly immersed myself into the college party scene. My thinking led me to believe that I might as well "go wild" because it was too late for me to be a "good girl" now. Partly due to shame and a good measure of insecurity, I lost much of my self-worth. I felt so stupid. Even worse, I felt used. But everything around me said my choice was normal.

The lifestyle was a vicious cycle. I needed to drink in order to lose my inhibitions, and then I had to drink some more in order to numb my pain.

So I assumed *I* was the one with the problem—the only one who felt ashamed, empty, and hurt.

This lifestyle, which the world around me cheered, was disappointing. Not wanting to be labeled the prude or uncool, I continued to live it up. In the campus party scene, "hooking up" with guys and drinking until dawn were normal. No one questioned this behavior. No one really considered the consequences or thought about the future. All that mattered was enjoying the buzz and meeting hot guys.

I was in the thick of it.

If you had looked at me, it would have seemed I was having a blast. I danced hard and laughed loud. And when it was time for the bars to close, I was the one looking for the "after party." But in reality, I was using alcohol and parties to mask the deep insecurity I felt. The lifestyle was a vicious cycle. I needed to drink in order to lose my inhibitions, and then I had to drink some more in order to numb my pain.

Graduating from college didn't change my life-style all that much. In fact, my partying only intensi-fied once I could get more than twenty dollars out of the ATM. My girlfriends and I were in the corporate world now. And in case you don't know, the two most important words in business aren't *debit* and *credit*. They are, in fact, *happy* and *hour*. I learned the power of these two words oh so quickly. Monday, Tuesday, and Wednesday, we actu-ally had to work. Drag. But Thursday and Friday, now that was a different story. These two days are set aside on the young business professional's calendar as sacred. Gone are the days of flirting with guys at fraternity mixers. Flirting is now called "networking" and is done over rounds of mixed drinks.

> As my partying accelerated, the fuel light on my soul began to blink a bright orange.

At some point in this journey I convinced myself I was having a good time. Whenever my emptiness sur-faced or the shame of my choices weighed down on me, I turned up the music, poured another glass, and tried to drown out the voice inside that whispered, "I still haven't found what I'm looking for." As my par-tying accelerated, the fuel light on my soul began to blink a bright orange. Feeling like I was running on empty, and desperate to fill the tank, I cranked up the intake of boys and booze.

Sex and the City

Moving from my college town to a big city also brought a whole new world of "opportunities" and a new set of role models. It was about this time that HBO released its soon-to-be-hit show *Sex and the City*. Today, thanks to syndication, these characters are household names: Carrie, Charlotte, Miranda, and Samantha. All over the city women began emulating the talk, walk, dress, and attitude portrayed on this show. We had sass. As independent single women, living by our own rules, we now had a show that spoke to the needs, wants, and questions of women.

But did it really?

Sex and the City became the show that defined life for modern single girls. It brought a whole new paradigm as to how women could live outside of the stereotypical roles of wives and mothers. For starters, *Sex and the City* taught us that women could be anything men could be. The characters fiercely defended women's rights to "have sex like a man." If men, they would say, could have sex without strings, then so could women. In fact, viewers were also told that we didn't need men. If you have a good group of girlfriends and a successful career, why would someone *need* a man?

These new role models also taught us that sex wasn't sacred; it was simply a biological function. It was "just sex." Sex shouldn't evoke feelings, and God forbid you be that girl who expected a commitment. *Sex and the City* also implied that only a silly girl still believed in marriage for a lifetime, and remaining faithful in a relationship was passé. Viewers were schooled in the fine art of seduction, which led me to believe that a woman's power was in her sexuality. These are but a few of the lessons learned from watching the show *Sex and the City*, and this new worldview on singleness was thought to be the pinnacle of success for women.

I looked into the empty martini glass I was holding and realized it was a great metaphor for my life.

Then why was I so miserable?

Night after night of living this way, I finally woke up. Sitting on a bar stool in a trendy club in the city, I looked into the empty martini glass I was holding and realized it was a great metaphor for my life. I was empty. I *still* hadn't found what I was looking for. I had the clothes, the career, the cute guys, and the world at my fingertips, but I was still, like my glass, empty. Each

Was I looking for Mr. Right or Mr. Right Now?

night when I went out with my girlfriends to the bars, I was searching for someone or something to fill my glass. Was I looking for Mr. Right or Mr. Right Now?

Honestly, I didn't know who I was or what I was looking for. But the longer I lived this way, one thing I knew for sure: I hadn't found *it*.

There had to be more to life than this.

After years of the *Sex and the City* lifestyle, I hadn't found happiness—I had found hardness. One can only give her soul away so many times before she begins putting up defensive armor against the pain. Slowly, over the years, I transformed. I became a woman I didn't recognize or like very much. The life that I was living promised to bring me pleasure and freedom, but the truth is, it did not deliver. Instead of pleasure, I found pain. Instead of freedom, I found despair. I was searching for a love that would make me whole, and instead I found shattered dreams. While the girl on the outside had changed dramatically, the true longings of my heart had never changed. Then one day, *The Love* for which my heart was longing found me.

A Love That Doesn't Hurt in the Morning

I was in my midtwenties when a friend invited me to visit her church. Church? Don't close the book! Those were my sentiments exactly, but then I reasoned, "Hmm . . . no booze but boys!" Oh yes! A whole new pool of pretties. Church boys. Finally, some upstanding men. Men with standards. Maturity. And most impor-

tantly, men new to me. Still on the prowl and ready
for the possibilities, I scrounged through my makeup
drawer looking for a halo, or at least a new M•A•C lipstick, and readied myself for a new singles scene. Most
go to a church to pray, but, clearly,
I was going to prey.

To my utter amazement, I did
meet a man, but this time, he
wasn't wearing khakis and a polo.
He was different from anyone I'd
ever met before. Magnetic. Mysteriously available.
Powerful and yet full of compassion. True. Kind. Revo-
lutionary. I was drawn to him. All of a sudden, I no
longer sat in my pew scanning the room for hotties.
Instead, I sat on the edge of my seat eager to hear more
about this man—this man named Jesus Christ.

> Most go to a
> church to pray,
> but, clearly, I was
> going to prey.

No one was more surprised by this turn of events
than me. I guess I thought the building would collapse
if a girl like me walked in. My view of God, especially
church, up to that point was about being good and
following rules. And as you know, I wasn't getting my
Ph.D. in either of these subjects. Had my girlfriend
not enticed me with the prospect of meeting a guy, I'm
sure I would have blown off her invitation. You see,
I'd grown up going to church only because my parents
required it. I knew religion, and all that did for me was
make me feel like a failure.

But what I didn't know was Jesus.

There I sat, a complete mess—and let's face it, with questionable motives—but hanging on every word. Something inside me stirred as I heard the message of God's love for me and His offer of forgiveness through Jesus Christ. Maybe I'd heard these words before, but for some reason this time it clicked. I guess my emptiness and the consequences of my choices opened my eyes to see my need for this new life God was offering me.

I came into a real relationship with Jesus—not rules or self-help but God Himself. The mercy of God wooed my heart, and slowly He transformed me into a new woman—a work I could never have done on my own. The hard edges, softened. The bitterness, sweetened. Anger turned to joy and despair to hope. What was broken became whole, and what was lost, restored. I finally found what I was looking for.

I was alive!

Jesus changed me from the inside out. Suddenly I had new desires. It's kind of hard to explain, but all of a sudden I recognized the emptiness of my former choices. Now, for the first time, I wanted to live for something greater than temporary pleasure. No more drinking to boost my confidence or scamming for guys to feel loved. My life no longer consisted of hook-ups, hangovers, and senseless heartbreaks.

Girls . . . let me just say, Jesus rocked my world!

Today, I've found the promises of God to be not only true but satisfying. Sure, I had my share of doubts, questions, and confusion at first, but the persistent love of God filled my emptiness and healed my wounded heart. I'd be lying if I told you every day is perfect or I never struggle, but the truth is I do know real joy. Unlike the temporary buzz of the *Sex and the City* days, this new life doesn't hurt in the morning.

Daylight is harsh on the self-esteem— banishing all remnants of false confidence with last night's moon.

What a contrast. Remember those mornings, girls? Morning breath and sobriety are a wicked cocktail. Far from feeling loved, living in the land of the casual "hook-up" causes a girl to feel more used than adored. Insecurity and regret usually show up about the time you make the proverbial walk of shame. Daylight is harsh on the self-esteem— banishing all remnants of false confidence with last night's moon.

I now realize that all of my life I was searching to fill my emptiness with men, margaritas, and Manolos, but nothing ever touched that deep place inside where my soul ached. And the more I tried to fill my soul with these things, the more disappointed I became. The reason these substitutes didn't satisfy is because my soul wasn't aching for alcohol or a man; my soul was aching for God.

I was just a girl searching for God. French philoso-pher Blaise Pascal once said, "There is a God-shaped vacuum in the heart of every man which cannot be filled by any created thing, but only by God Himself." Here Pascal addressed Bono's dilemma and my own as well. The reason I hadn't found what I was looking for in that guy's dorm room was because my soul wasn't searching for a man—my soul was searching for God. And like Bono, my God-shaped vacuum required something that no relationship, earthly pleasure, or material possession could ever fill. And that, my friend, is why I want to uncover *the rest of the story.*

Looking
for Love in All
the Wrong Places

Do women just really want to be rescued?

CARRIE BRADSHAW OF *SEX AND THE CITY*

Season 3, episode 31, "Where There's Smoke There's Fire"

*A*fter a hard night on the town, the women of *Sex and the City* hit their local breakfast spot to dish on the previous evening's events and the men it involved. The night before, Carrie, as a local celebrity of sorts, was called upon to judge a firefighters' calendar contest on Staten Island. One ferry ride and several Staten Island Iced Teas later, the girls found themselves in foreign territory. Samantha, of course, was enamored with the smokin' hot body of one of the firemen, while Carrie met a handsome politician who had the hots for her. Charlotte indulged in one too many cocktails, and as a result she is nursing quite a headache the next morning.

Back on the island—Manhattan, that is—their get-together results in a lively discussion of the topic "Why do women love firemen?" Miranda leads the charge with her observations, and the others follow suit. Their conversation is the typical brunch banter until Charlotte chimes in with her reason, bringing the table to a stunned silence: "Women just really want to be rescued." She sighs as she props up her aching head with her hands. You could hear a pin drop as the other women stare back at her in disbelief. *Did she really just say that?* At this point Carrie, in a voice-over, describes Charlotte's comment as "the statement single women in their thirties are never supposed to think, much less say out loud."

The Girls

Just in case you aren't familiar with the show (or you've been watching PBS for the last decade), let me give you a little 411 on the girls of *Sex and the City*. Carrie Bradshaw writes a column about sex and relationships in New York City. Carrie is fashionable and witty, and her love life is the catalyst for the show's plotline. No one captures the plight of the love-seeking single woman better than Carrie Bradshaw. She uses her own dating experiences as material for her column, and she is not one to shy away from difficult or taboo subjects. Carrie is real—real about her desires and real about her weaknesses. Somehow through it all she still hopes to find real love. Carrie's escapades as a single woman in New York include her three best friends: Samantha, Miranda, and Charlotte.

Samantha Jones is a powerful NYC publicist who brings the shock factor to the group as she relates her sexual conquests to the girls. Samantha wears shamelessness as a badge of honor. Sam Jones is a successful woman who knows what she wants—and most of the time she gets it. On the outside she radiates confidence in everything. Although there are moments that reveal serious cracks in her armor, for the most part Samantha seems to relish in her lifestyle. She embraces uninhibited sexuality with a varied (and large) group of men. Forget wedding dreams; Samantha is one to choose lust over love any night, and she's proud of it. The only thing Sam fears is a *real* relationship.

Next we have the practical and very serious Miranda Hobbs. Miranda is smart, self-assured, and proud of her achievements. She is driven, be it in her professional or personal life. She made partner in her law firm and bought her own apartment on the Upper West Side. However, like the other women, she struggles with her love life. At times, Miranda has abandoned the pursuit of love altogether. Known as the tough girl, she doesn't open up easily, masking her vulnerability with cynicism and self-deprecating humor about life and love.

Charlotte York is an art gallery curator who is portrayed to be prudish (by the show's standards) when it comes to sex but hasn't lost her faith in finding "the one." Charlotte has an optimistic outlook on love and romance amid the ever-complex dating scene of NYC. Well bred, she walks through life with a perfect sense of decorum and a good dose of idealism. For years Charlotte has maintained a clear vision of the life she's wanted. First and foremost, she wants to get married. She wants true love. And she wants her husband to be wealthy and handsome and to belong to the social elite.

In this particular episode, "Where There's Smoke There's Fire," each character deals with the desire to be "rescued" in her own stereotypical style. Charlotte, believing a man will solve all of life's problems, vows that this is the year she will *finally* get married. She complains to her girlfriends, "I've been dating since I was fifteen. I'm exhausted! Where is he?" So in this episode, Charlotte goes in search of the man she hopes will be her Prince Charming. But alas, the prince she meets while out with Carrie one night is less than charming. For Charlotte, the search for the white knight continues.

Carrie, on the other hand, still struggling from a recent breakup, turns to her beloved Jimmy Choos as her lifesaver. Deciding "to rescue her ankles from a life of boredom," in typical Carrie fashion, she maxes out her credit card and goes shopping, hoping to fix all that ails her. I have to ask, how many pairs of shoes does it take to rescue a woman?

Meanwhile Miranda is in need of a *real* rescue, but her self-reliant attitude rises to the surface and keeps her from asking for help. She views the need to be rescued as a

> How many pairs of shoes does it take to rescue a woman?

weakness. Miranda takes independence to an extreme and refuses to let her boyfriend Steve assist her after her eye surgery. In fear of appearing needy, she'd rather risk her health than accept Steve's offer of assistance, but luckily he comes to her aid despite her protests. Miranda's way of dealing with the desire to be rescued is a simple one: denial.

Samantha tackles her "rescue" fantasy through her characteristic way: sex. Void of sentiments or emotional need, Sam hopes sexual pleasure will rescue her. While visiting her current fling, the fireman she met at the calendar contest, Samantha seeks to fulfill her own fireman fantasy. To her alarm, the fire station siren blares while she is naked, leaving her abandoned to find her clothes when her "hero" is called away to a real emergency. This episode reveals (quite literally) that Samantha's choice leaves her exposed, alone, and ashamed. I wonder, *Is this the fairy tale she always dreamed of?*

The Confession

Knowing that Charlotte is the hopeful romantic of the bunch, it comes as no surprise to us that she utters the words that "single women in their thirties are never supposed to think, much less say out loud." Of course, she is the one to confess, "Women just really want to be rescued." But what's the big deal? Did she say something wrong? Why are the others so shocked? Is Charlotte still drunk? Or maybe, just maybe, she has stumbled onto something. Do women *really* long to be rescued? Is there something deep down inside each of us that would love to have the white knight sweep in and carry us away? I think for most girls the answer is, "Yes!"

Recently I watched the hit show *The Bachelor*. This particular season the bachelor happened to be a real prince. Fighting for his affection and attention were twenty-five beautiful women. In the two-hour premiere, one common theme resonated from the women: they wanted the fairy tale. As the evening progressed and the alcohol flowed, the women revealed more and more of their hearts' true desires. Each wanted to be chosen by the prince and for her childhood longings of being a princess to come true. As I watched the episode and listened to their comments, I thought, *This is* reality *television*. Hungering for love and desiring to be chosen, these women had picked up their lives and moved to a castle in Rome in hopes of being rescued by Prince Charming.

So why did the *Sex and the City* characters, and perhaps many of us, bristle at Charlotte's comment? It seems the other characters are much too independent and savvy to admit this inner longing. They pride themselves on self-sufficiency and hope to evolve past any notions of having needs and longings, so they blast Charlotte's old-fashioned idea with a dose of reality. Reality, according to Miranda, is that "the white knight only exists in the movies." Her reply rings with bitterness toward men and a lack of trust in anyone but herself. The same is true of Carrie's response, except she takes a different approach, saying, "Did you ever think we're supposed to rescue ourselves?" There it is—the motto of the modern single woman: "I don't need anyone, and I can do it all by myself."

Charlotte does not buy their dismissals, and her response to their advice is revealing when she replies, "That's depressing!" And we have to admit, it is, but why? Probably because as women, since the first time we played with Barbie, we've imagined Ken coming in his sports car to rescue her from the clutches of GI Joe. This is part of the fabric of being a girl. But surely, some would say, we've all grown up and put those childish dreams behind us. After all, hasn't life taught us some pretty tough lessons? White knights don't always come to the rescue, and sometimes, let's face it, Ken *actually* likes GI Joe. For some of us, these life lessons have left us hard and a little jaded too. So, like Miranda, it's easier to shove the desire to be rescued behind us and pretend it's just a fantasy.

But what if it's not? Let's imagine just for a moment that it's real—the fairy tale, the hero, and all the stuff that romantic movies thrive on. Let's imagine for just a minute that it is a legitimate longing and examine why Charlotte's confession resonates with us. Why *do* women long to be rescued? Why is this desire ingrained in the heart of every little girl? To answer this question, we must dig a little deeper and ask some fundamental questions.

The Rescue

First, what is meant by the word *rescue?* The word *rescue* means "to set free, as from danger or imprisonment; to save." (Kudos, Mr. Webster.) From the damsel in distress, who is tied to train tracks as a high-speed locomotive approaches, to the princess, who is locked away in the perilous castle, the role of the hero is to save his lady from whatever enemy she faces.

I'll be honest: life's been so intense at times that I've daydreamed that someone comes along and takes me away from it all. I've gazed out my office window hoping to see Prince Charming ride up on his white horse (or in an SUV—I'm not really picky about the mode of transportation). Just like Charlotte, I did my share of barhopping in the past, hoping to meet "the one." But I've realized the desire to be rescued goes much deeper than just a longing for a man. I know plenty of women with great men who still

Our desire to be rescued implies we are held captive . . . imprisoned.

have this desire. Women identify with the longing to be rescued—young and old, married and single, rich and poor. Ladies, this desire is bigger than any man can fill—yes, it is even bigger than Mr. Big.

Because this is a common desire, is there also then a common problem? In other words, is there something that we all need to be rescued *from?* Is there something basic to all of us that causes us to feel like we need help or we need to be set free? What is it that makes us hope and dream that someone will come along who can make all right in our world? Our desire to be rescued implies we are held captive . . . imprisoned.

But what is this prison?

I believe the universal prison in which we are all held is best described in a country song from the '80s by Waylon Jennings called "Lookin' for Love in All the Wrong Places." (Pardon if my country girl roots show through for a bit—we'll be back to the land of five-dollar coffee and stilettos shortly.) Now, you might remember this song from John Travolta's hit movie *Urban Cowboy* (he was totally robbed on the awards that year, by the way). Whatever your history with this song, I'm here to tell you, it is truth! The prison that each of us needs to be rescued from is one of "Looking for Love in All the Wrong Places."

The Prison

As a child of the '80s (a decade of great fashion and even greater music), I grew up singing the words into my hairbrush microphone. But it wasn't until years later, in the '90s (now wearing grunge and listening to Nirvana—thankfully that trend was short lived), that I realized just how dead-on these lyrics are about life and love. One might say they are . . . *profound*. The song is a classic because everyone can identify with the problem. Here's the point: this song describes, and human experience confirms, that humankind is in a prison—a perpetual and fruitless search for something or someone to make us feel loved, complete, and whole. Each one of us has an empty place in our hearts that aches to be filled.

You know the ache I'm talking about. You aren't satisfied; you don't feel complete; something is missing, and you keep hoping that the next relationship or the next job or even a new outfit will remedy the ache, but it doesn't. Life can be going along great, and, yet, that empty gnawing is still there—the one that cries out, "I still haven't found what I'm looking for!" And as a result, we desperately search and we hunt for a love that will fill our emptiness and make us feel complete. And on and on and on we go.

Happy hour eventually is over, the guy inevitably fails to be perfect, and food may fill a stomach but not a soul.

This is my story. I went looking for love in all kinds of places, only to find myself more empty and confused as a result. From parties to people, from shopping to men, job promotions and even more parties . . . hoping something would bring me a sense of security or love. Happy hour eventually is over, the guy inevitably fails to be perfect, and food may fill a stomach but not a soul. My disillusionment eventually led to despair. Life seemed without hope and joy seemed elusive. I was captive to the emptiness.

I see this same desperation and disappointment in the lives of the women portrayed on the show *Sex and the City*. While on the surface everything appears glamorous and exciting, if you take a step back and evaluate their soul-searching questions, you see women who are hoping for someone to rescue them from the pain and emptiness they feel.

I was captive to the emptiness.

For example, let's consider Charlotte. Like most of us girls, she hopes to find the love her heart longs for in a man. She is by far the most hopeful romantic of the crew. Over the six seasons of *Sex and the City*, we watched as she searched from man to man hoping to find "the one" who would *complete* her. Did she find him? Well, yes and no. She did get married (two times, in fact), but once she found a husband, did he fill her emptiness? No. The last season ended with Charlotte hoping the ache in her heart would be filled with a child. So, her search continues.

Can you relate? How often do you tell yourself the following?

- *If I were married, then my life would be perfect.*
- Or, *If I had a better job, then I would be satisfied.*
- Or, *When I buy my own house, then I will be happy.*
- Or what about this one? *When I lose ten pounds, then I will feel OK.*

We believe the solution to the restlessness we feel is remedied by finding something or someone to fill the emptiness in our hearts. But as we all know, those things may work for a season, but after a while that old familiar ache returns and we move on to the next thing or the next person, thinking that this time we will find what we are looking for.

This is why I call "looking for love in all the wrong places" a prison. For some of us it can be a life sentence. The pursuit to fill the void can be endless and full of disappointment. But that leads us to the most important question of all: what caused this emptiness in the first place?

The answer is found in the Bible. Yes, I said the Bible. (You know, the best-selling book of all time? Yes, that's the one I'm talking about.) In Scripture we are told the story of God and how our problem of "looking for love" first began. The Bible tells us that humanity is created by God and for God. Translation: He is the Designer and Creator of Life, so in order to find out how things got all jacked up in our world, we must go back to the "Designer's manual."

Let's play *Fantasy Island* for just a minute and imagine Dolce & Gabana designs a one-of-a-kind outfit just for you. It goes without saying that they would know best how this outfit is supposed to be worn (the perfect accessories, fit, shoes, etc.). Why? Because they are the designers. Hello? That's the same with God. As our Creator, we need to look to Him and His Word (a.k.a. The Bible) to understand how life was meant to be lived. So for us to understand why we deal with insecurity, self-doubt, restlessness, and a perpetually empty soul, we must turn to the original design to see what God created us for and what went wrong.

The Beginning

In Genesis, the first book of the Bible, we find that after five quite productive days of speaking into existence solar systems and farm animals and the oceans and the assorted sea creatures that would fill them, God then turned His creative eye to bring into existence the crown jewel of His creation: humankind.

> *God spoke: "Let us make human beings in our*
> *image, make them reflecting our nature."*
> *God formed Man out of dirt from the ground and*
> *blew into his nostrils the breath of life. The*
> *Man came alive—a living soul!*
> *God looked over everything he had made;*
> *it was so good, so very good!*
> Genesis 1:26; 2:7; 1:31 (MSG)

In the beginning, God placed the human race in a beautiful garden that He filled with everything they needed for a life of joy, peace, and purpose. Adam and Eve were provided for and given the responsibility to rule over and care for God's creation. And right from the start, God declared our identity (the "who am I?" question) when He looked on the first man and woman and declared us to be "very good" (Gen. 1:31).

This is a powerful moment. When God speaks over Adam and Eve the word *good*, He establishes their identity. You know how when you fall in love, one of the best things about being with that special person is how they make you feel about yourself? Well, that is the situation we have here. Our God-given design is one that when we are in relationship with Him, we know who we are and we know we are loved. As the Designer, He alone has the authority to name and define—and His declaration of His design from the very beginning was "very good."

Here's the thing: originally humankind didn't need to be rescued from "looking for love in all the wrong places." Why not, you ask? Because all was right and good in our world—we didn't struggle with the self-doubt, insecurity, restlessness, and emptiness that you and I experience today. You see, it was never God's original design for people to suffer from the nagging inadequacies we feel.

The Bible describes God's original design of man and woman in a physically descriptive way, which, in truth, speaks to their emotional, psychological, and spiritual condition as well. "The two of them, the Man and his Wife, were naked, but they felt no shame" (Gen. 2:25 MSG).

Perhaps you are imagining a hippie nudist colony in the middle of a tree orchard. Maybe this is not your ideal living situation, and I can totally understand your hesitation. The point of the Scripture is not to endorse a clothing-optional lifestyle; the purpose of this text is to explain the pure freedom and confidence that Adam and Eve knew in God's original design.

The Design

Uncovered. Naked and not ashamed! This is the condition of man and woman while living in the midst of the unconditional love of God. Adam and Eve didn't know the meaning of insecurity. They didn't ask questions such as, "Am I good enough? Am I pretty enough? Will I be accepted? Am I lovable?" Eve never asked, "Does this fig leaf make me look fat?"

Eve never asked, "Does this fig leaf make me look fat?"

Identity is something that is bestowed. We cannot define ourselves. Today, we are always looking outside of ourselves for someone to tell us who we are, but for Adam and Eve, the question of their identity wasn't up for debate. First of all, when God created them, He essentially said, "You are good and you don't need to do anything to prove yourself or seek anyone else to tell you that you are worthy of love." So, for Adam and Eve, the self-worth question was solved. If the God of the universe, who spoke the world into existence, said they were *good*—then that settled it.

Girlfriends, can you fathom walking into a room and never thinking, *Do I look OK?* Just imagine being fully known, explicitly seen, and fully loved—never fearing rejection, never meeting a new group of people and feeling like you don't belong. Try to imagine having a confidence that isn't based on fickle things such as money, a new pair of shoes, or attracting male attention. Or better yet, what if Carrie didn't need fashion, Samantha sex, Charlotte a husband, or Miranda her career?

> *The state of being "naked and not ashamed" implies that they were free to be themselves—without props, without additives, without labels, without pretense.*

The other reason Adam and Eve were so secure is that they lived in the presence of the One who *is* love. God "is love" we are told in the Bible; love, defined as seeking the best for others. Because God is the Author of Life and the Giver of all things, He alone is the ultimate expression of love. Love is life giving, and that is exactly who God is.

Adam and Eve lived in the presence of His perfect love, so they had no reason to go searching for anything—because they didn't know what it was to feel empty. The state of being "naked and not ashamed" implies that they were free to be themselves—without props, without additives, without labels, without pretense. Because they lived in the unconditional love of God, they were secure and they knew they were accepted simply for who they were.

So, for the million-dollar question: what went wrong?

The Scam

The pure freedom and unshakable confidence Adam and Eve experienced were wonderful while they lasted, but the harmony and beauty of Eden were shattered when Satan entered the scene. Previously, God told Adam and Eve that everything in the garden was theirs for enjoyment. Unparalleled beauty. Ultimate bliss. Everything in the Garden of Eden was good for Adam and Eve, except for one thing: "the tree of the knowledge of good and evil." This particular tree was off limits. God told them not to eat of it, for if they did, they would die (Gen. 2:16–17).

Is God a divine fun thwarter, or was there a reason they couldn't eat of this tree? Here's the problem: the "tree of the knowledge of good and evil" represented independence from God. The tree itself was fine, but taking the forbidden fruit placed man in a role he was never designed to play—that is, the role of determining for himself what is good and what is evil. God is the all-creating, all-sustaining, all-defining, all-powerful One. He has the authority to define reality, for He alone is God.

But as we see in the following passage, Satan (starring as the Serpent) scammed Eve into disobeying God. This deception is the root cause of our perpetual search for love and completion today—the real reason we are looking for love in all the wrong places and we all long to be rescued.

> *The serpent was clever, more clever than*
> *any wild animal GOD had made. He spoke to the*
> *Woman: "Do I understand that God told you not*
> *to eat from any tree in the garden?"*
>
> *The Woman said to the serpent, "Not at all.*
> *We can eat from the trees in the garden. It's only*
> *about the tree in the middle of the garden that*
> *God said, 'Don't eat from it; don't even touch it*
> *or you'll die.'"*
>
> *The serpent told the Woman, "You won't die.*
> *God knows that the moment you eat from that*
> *tree, you'll see what's really going on. You'll be*
> *just like God, knowing everything, ranging all*
> *the way from good to evil."*
>
> *When the Woman saw that the tree looked*
> *like good eating and realized what she would get*
> *out of it—she'd know everything!—she took and*
> *ate the fruit and then gave some to her husband,*
> *and he ate.* Genesis 3:1–6 (MSG)

I'll give it to Satan; he's a good salesman. He offered Eve something pretty enticing when he told her, "You will be just like God." Wow—what an incredible offer! But like my mom always said, "If something sounds too good to be true, it probably is." And in this case, the old saying is right.

Satan tricked Eve. But it is important to note just exactly how this ruse went down. First, he caused her to doubt God by asking, "Did God really say?" Then he outright called God a liar when he suggested, "Surely, you won't die." By leading Eve to doubt the truthfulness of God's word, Satan undermined her trust in God.

The serpent called God a liar, and Eve now faced a choice: believe God or believe Satan. So, the great deceiver appealed to her physical senses and gave her ample reasons to buy his con: the forbidden fruit was good for food, able to make one wise, and the ultimate temptation—to be one's own god. Satan's lure implied freedom, power, control . . . but in reality, the opposite occurred. (Personally, I'd love it if we could TIVO history. I'd hit rewind. Go back to the beginning, and have a little heart-to-heart with my sister Eve.) I digress. Where was I? Oh yes, the scam.

Satan's scam was basically an attack on the goodness of God. His theory went something like this: if God is good, then He would allow you to eat of any tree. God must be *bad* because He said you can't eat of this certain tree.

Think back for a minute to your high school days. Remember when your parents said you couldn't date that certain guy? Remember how you thought they were flat-out evil incarnate and surely they were plotting to ruin your life? But now, you look back and realize your parents were right—that guy wasn't the best for you. In this scenario protection = love.

The same is true of our relationship with God. Here's the thing: God knows what is best for us. But as we see, Satan distorts God's protective provision to be a bad thing, and Eve bought into the lie. She rebelled against her God—her source of life, security, and love.

Perhaps you've been in a similar situation. You hear a great marketing pitch about a new cosmetic product that promises to eliminate wrinkles, cellulite, bad breath, and make you taller all at the same time. Sold, you charge the wonder pill to your credit card (at only $49.99 a month for the rest of your life) only later to discover . . . you've been scammed! The whole thing is a lie. The wonder pill isn't so wonderful. It doesn't deliver on its promises, and with it comes a whole new world of side effects. This is exactly like Satan's promise to Eve, except the side effects of his scam were far more devastating—they were life altering.

Today, many women, like Eve, are deceived—believing the lie that the love we hunger for is found in the alluring lifestyle portrayed on *Sex and the City*. Masked behind couture fashion, clever writing, and beautiful people is a life of searching and desperation. I know because I've been there myself. The lure is clever, but the promises don't deliver. Here's the big problem with deception: you don't know it's a lie until you face the consequences.

Here's the big problem with deception: you don't know it's a lie until you face the consequences.

The Loss

The sad fact is that Adam and Eve were deceived, but the even sadder reality is that they lost the very thing that made them feel whole, complete, and secure: their relationship with God, their Creator. Separated from their source of confidence and estranged from the Giver of Life, they covered themselves with leaves and tried to hide from God.

Now, "naked" doesn't imply freedom; it exposes. Vulnerable, ashamed, and confused, they realized something *big* was missing, and that something was God. In choosing to be their own God, Adam and Eve fell into shame. Their inadequacy to fill God's shoes was clear, and the shame enveloped them like a fog. So they hid.

We were not created for life separated from God. When Adam and Eve chose to dethrone God and cut the cord of dependence—by deciding for themselves what is good and evil—humankind indeed got independence from God. And this independence is the source of every heartache, disappointment, and the emptiness we experience in the world today.

Recently, as I flipped through TV channels, I came across a documentary about a baby inside a mother's womb. (Note to self—epidural!) Riveting television. The miracle of life is breathtaking. I sat for hours as the commentator explained the stages of growth and development preceding birth. The most interesting thing I learned about in the wee hours of the morning was the perfect environment that the child inhabits—the mother's womb. In the womb a baby is nourished, sheltered, protected, and literally attached to his source of life.

This got me to thinking. That's a lot like the state of humankind in the garden with God before evil entered the world. Everything we needed was supplied. And there we, too, were connected to our *true* source of life. So, for us to fully comprehend what we've lost, imagine a child taken from the womb, separated from his mother, and left without anyone to feed, protect, or care for him. You might think I'm being a bit dramatic, but this comes as close to illustrating the weight of our loss as anything I know. Simply, we weren't designed for life apart from God.

Today, we all experience the loss and separation that resulted from Adam and Eve's fatal decision. Instead of knowing peace and security, we feel angst and incompleteness. Instead of knowing who we are and if we are loved, we are constantly searching and striving for someone to tell us who we are. Our desire to be rescued, therefore, finds its origin in the human need to be reconnected with our Creator—to be back in the place of security and rest that comes from being in His presence—simply, the place we were created to inhabit.

Charlotte is right. Women really do want to be rescued!

The Rest of the Story

I'm just a girl who believed the lie that the deep longings of my soul could be fulfilled in the lifestyle portrayed on *Sex and the City*. Rescued from the emptiness, I'm here to tell other women *the rest of the story*. God doesn't abandon us. He knows our design. He knows apart from Him we are searching, restless, and incomplete. And because He loves us with this incomprehensible love, He comes to rescue us and set us free from our prison of "looking for love in all the wrong places."

Hang tight; we will discover the rest of that story later.

Before we uncover God's amazing solution, we need to take a closer look at our problem. In the following chapters we will examine the various ways we, and the women of *Sex and the City*, attempt to fill this God-shaped hole in our souls. We will discover how these methods are not only inadequate but most of the time destructive. Disconnected from our true Source of love, life, and identity, we turn to these substitutes, hoping they will fill the void. Hear me out; some of these can be good things (relationships, food, sex, careers, success, friendships), but whenever we try to put anything in the place that is intended for God alone, the inadequacy of the substitute becomes painfully obvious. Frustrated and yet still empty, we turn to the next trinket, the next person, or the next pleasure . . . and all along our journey, that small voice inside each of us whispers, "I still haven't found what I'm looking for."

chapter three

Looking for Love in Mr. Right

I've been dating since I was fifteen.
Where is he? My hair hurts!
CHARLOTTE YORK OF *SEX AND THE CITY*
Season 3, episode 31, "Where There's Smoke There's Fire"

Charlotte York is a woman who knows exactly what she wants. As Carrie once said, "Charlotte treated marriage like a sorority she was desperately hoping to pledge." She, far more than any other character on *Sex and the City*, desires a husband. Not just any husband: The One, Her Soul Mate, Mr. Right, the one with whom she will live happily ever after. Charlotte wants the fairy tale, and she is not ashamed to admit it. In one particular episode, Charlotte declares this to be the year that she will *finally* get married. To this thirty-something woman, the tick of the biological clock is beginning to sound like the gong of Big Ben. Needless to say, Charlotte is ready to meet her man.

As a smart and successful single woman, Charlotte isn't one to just sit back and let life happen; she has a plan! Her quest for her own holy grail will be accomplished through strategy and skillful planning. Over brunch, of course, Charlotte informs the others that she is reading a new book, *Marriage Incorporated: How to Apply Successful Business Strategies to Finding a Husband*. This book encourages professional women to approach finding a mate with the same dedication and organization that they bring to their careers. This information brings an eye roll from Miranda, a snarl from Samantha, and a shrug from Carrie, who describes Charlotte as "a professional husband hunter" (season 3, episode 37, "Drama Queens").

We may laugh at Charlotte's husband-hunting tactics. We may feel a sense of embarrassment for her and roll our eyes with Miranda; but deep down, most of us girls secretly know that at some point we, too, have gone on a manhunt. I'll be honest. As much as Charlotte's desperation embarrasses me for my entire gender, I know that I've done some manhunting of my own. I'd like to invite you to take a trip down memory lane with me, into my *Sex and the City* past, as I recall a "hunting season" of my own.

The Manhunt

Music blaring and drinks flowing, the pre-party to the evening's manhunt was by now a ritual. The first order of business: alcohol. Typically, a night on the town with the girls began with drinking at home in order to be fun and friendly when you actually arrived at the club. But far more important than the drinking, the biggest decision of all must be made: what to wear. This is huge, really. So much is at stake. Seriously, more time went into this decision than most of us spent deciding which college we would attend. So from this brain trust arose carefully crafted ensembles—pulled together from the various wardrobes and push-up bras on hand—to form for each girl the ultimate man-hunting outfit.

After choosing the perfect outfit, we then moved on to the next order of business: where should we go hunting tonight? To a dance club, a rave, a house party, or just a regular bar . . . so many options. Some nights it depended on our mood, and other nights it depended on who was going to be where. But really, in the end there was a simple formula:

single guys + (free) alcohol = desired hunting ground

The higher a place scored using this finely tuned formula, the more likely it was that you would find us flocking to this location like bears to honey.

Most nights out on the town followed this typical pattern. The planning stage, which I have briefly described, was followed by what I like to call "the hunt." Now, we would probably never admit it, but we went out with one agenda: to meet guys. I know it sounds pathetic, and, frankly, I'm really embarrassed to write it; but honestly, that was what most nights boiled down to: getting dressed up, going out to a bar, and hoping to meet someone.

We could walk into a club and in a matter of two minutes size up the prospects with a discerning eye. Like a military surveillance team, we could sweep through the place and report back to one another with a rundown of the cute, hot, and need-to-avoid status of every male in the room. We were women on a mission. I'm not saying this was a rational or logical mission, but the underlying purpose of the mission was to hopefully meet someone and well . . . you know . . . become the next Carrie and Mr. Big (minus all of his obvious commitment problems). The fuel of hope that kept us going out night after night was always the chance that just maybe, this time, we would find the love we were looking for.

I find it quite ironic that bars are the number-one place people go to in hopes of finding love—the irony being that a bar is a place you go to get a drink. I wonder . . . *Is there a connection? Why is it that in a place where people go to satisfy a physical thirst, you have people flocking to find a solution to a much deeper thirst, their thirst for love?* Hmm . . . thoughts to ponder.

Thirsty

When was the last time you were super thirsty? I mean like totally parched. Take just a second and remember that feeling—the sheer desperation of needing something to quench your thirst. It brings to mind the image of a lone traveler in a desert gazing into the horizon in search of a cool spring. I've never had to crawl across the desert, but I think the thirstiest I've ever been was during college when I worked at a summer camp for kids. It was fun but swelteringly hot outside. The heat alone was one factor, but, also, the many activities we did during the day made me primed for dehydration. Running, swimming, hiking, sports competitions—by midafternoon my throat was raw and lips cracked. On multiple occasions I remember being tempted to drink water straight from the fishing pond because my thirst was so painful.

Each afternoon one of the counselors walked around the camp to the various work stations bearing cold drinks. One particular summer, my afternoon assignment found me the last stop on the cold drink run. Inevitably, the only thing left was a hot, syrupy soda. It never failed. I took the Dr. Pepper—or even worse, grape soda—and in my moment of desperation tilted my head back and took a long drink. For a minute, the need was gone. But just as quickly, my thirst was back and raging with a vengeance. Only one thing was going to satisfy and that was the genuine article: H_2O. I was in desperate need of the real thing.

As I think about how intense my thirst was during those long, hot days, I can't help but see the similarity between my body's thirst for real water and my soul's thirst for God. But just like settling for a hot soda instead of cool, refreshing water, for years I settled for what I hoped would satisfy my thirst: a man. So time and time again, I hoped a relationship would fulfill the deepest longings in my soul—but like the hot soda, the hot guy worked for a moment, but in the end I was left parched.

Relationships

Let me explain. Relationships can be amazing, especially at the beginning—they hold so much promise. You meet a guy, and if there's actually a connection—or as Carrie would say, "that za za zoom"—there is so much hope and excitement when you two first start hanging out. Often we enter these relationships with a secret thirst, not a physical one, but our souls are thirsty and we hope certain needs will be quenched in the relationship.

We come into a relationship hoping to feel that we **belong** to someone. And for a season, we do feel that way. There's that rush that happens when we walk down the street hand in hand or the joy of having a date for our office Christmas party—or just fill in the blank for your particular can't-go-alone event. The confident feeling that says, "I'm with someone" makes us feel important, special, and desired.

So time and time again, I hoped a relationship would fulfill the deepest longings in my soul—but like the hot soda, the hot guy worked for a moment, but in the end I was left parched.

We also come into relationships with the hope of finding **acceptance**—someone who will love us, as one of my favorite movie lines says, "Just as you are." (Thank you very much, *Bridgette Jones*.) We hope the nagging questions about our worth, our lovability, and all those pesky self-doubts will be removed with the mere presence of another.

Many of us enter into a relationship and think, *Security at last! Finally, someone who will make everything OK. I'm not alone anymore.* Perhaps subconsciously we believe we've found someone who will take care of us and meet all of our needs.

And last, but certainly not least, we come into relationships with a deep thirst for **completion**. This is the hope that someone else will fill our emptiness

45

and drive away the loneliness. Oh yes, romantic love comes in a rush, and let's face it . . . romance *is* a rush. But there still comes a day when we wake up and realize, "I'm still empty." We still don't feel all that secure. For some reason we don't feel loved. And even if there is a head on the pillow next to ours, we can still feel completely alone.

Simply put, we come into relationships looking for **unconditional love**. But can this love be found in any human relationship? Or better yet, are human relationships enough to satisfy the thirst of our souls for belonging, security, acceptance, and completion? Can boyfriends or husbands banish all of our insecurities and make us feel whole and complete? I would suggest the answer is no.

For many women the disappointment can lead to disillusionment—is the love my heart thirsts for really available? Disillusionment can send some women into depression and even others to divorce. I'm serious. Think about it. If I enter a relationship with the expectation that this guy is going to fill my soul and drive away all my insecurities, what happens when he fails? Does that mean I married the wrong guy? Does that mean I haven't found "The One"? Granted, there are reasonable expectations we should hold as a part of being in a healthy relationship—one in which both parties are concerned with meeting the other person's needs. And if a man is a real man, he will be concerned with making his girl feel secure, accepted, and loved.

But the point is this: even the best guy, on his best day, can go only so far. There will always remain a place, unreachable by flowers and kisses, that belongs to God alone; and it is in this place, the God-spot, that our deepest thirst is found. And until that place is filled by God Himself, all the romance in the world will never satisfy.

> *There will always remain a place, unreachable by flowers and kisses, that belongs to God alone; and it is in this place, the God-spot, that our deepest thirst is found.*

One stop at your local grocery store will confirm this truth. Pick up a *People, US Weekly*, or any of the other celebrity gossip magazines, and you will find tales of souls searching for love. Our addiction to these publications is fueled by who's dating whom, who's divorced whom, and why-did-so-and-so-leave-her-latest-soulmate drama. When the celebrity relationship begins, each party is gushing to the world as to how they've found the one, the love of their lives. But then, it seems that no sooner have you thrown out the last week's edition, the celebrity has moved on to someone new, someone who will hopefully, this time, meet all his or her needs and quench the thirst. What we call mindless entertainment is simply a parade of thirsty souls (lavished in over-the-top gifts, gestures, and dramatic declarations to Oprah) looking for love.

It goes without saying that no *Sex and the City* character typifies the lovelorn woman better than Carrie Bradshaw. Throughout the six seasons, Carrie's love life is the central focus of the show's plotline. Her hopes, dreams, and disappointments fuel much of *Sex and the City's* success with women everywhere. Why do women love Carrie? Is it just her love for shoes? Is it the fashion? Perhaps, but I think the real reason we love Carrie is we identify with her struggles, her desires, and her hope to find real love.

In the final two episodes of *Sex and the City*, Carrie's search for love has led her from the comfy confines of her New York City apartment across the Atlantic Ocean to an exquisite hotel room in Paris to be with her current "luvah," Alexander Petrovsky. In what is one of the most dramatic moments of the six seasons of *Sex and the City*, Miss Bradshaw confesses the ultimate desire of her heart:

> *I'm looking for love.*
>
> *Real love. Ridiculous, inconvenient, consuming, can't-live-without-each-other love.*
>
> *And I don't think that love is here in this expensive suite in this lovely hotel in Paris.*
>
> Season 6, episode 94, "American Girl in Paris—Part Deux"

With these words Carrie ends her love affair with The Russian, who is yet another disappointment in her quest to find "real love." If you saw this episode, you probably felt the weight of Carrie's disappointment. Carrie kissed her friends good-bye and left life in New York behind . . . and for what? Yet another failed relationship. She's broken and hurting—her heart is ripped open—and we wonder if she will ever find what she's looking for.

The writers of *Sex and the City* know viewers love a happy ending, so how else would Carrie's quest for real love end than by her being reunited with her long-time love, Mr. Big, who now seems to be finally and miraculously ready to commit to the relationship. True to Hollywood form, the final scene reveals a carefree Carrie, strolling down the streets of her beloved New York City answering a call from her love, Mr. Big, whose name we finally learn is John. The two are now living happily ever after . . . or so it seems.

The Rest of the Story

As the credits rolled on the last episode of *Sex and the City*, I found myself asking a question: what is the rest of the story? Did these two actually make it down the aisle? Was Big really able to overcome his fear of intimacy and give of himself in a relationship? And if so, was Carrie finally content once the chase was over and she had him as her own? Did Carrie actually find the love that she desired in her relationship with Mr. Big? Did they really live happily ever after? Because this story is fiction, the answers will always lie in our imagination.

Carrie's love life chronicles the plight of many women. Like you and me, she is desperately looking for love. But what I see in Carrie and her friends on *Sex and the City* is hauntingly familiar. I've seen it in myself and in my girlfriends, and it is a blatant case of a misplaced hope.

> *My marriage is a fake Fendi!*
> Charlotte York of Sex and the City

The Design

When Carrie Bradshaw stands before Alexander (a.k.a. The Russian) and proclaims her heart's desire for real love, she echoes a longing of women everywhere. I know because I want the same thing. Who doesn't want to be loved? So, as we uncover the problem of looking for love in relationships, I want to be clear right from the start: there is nothing wrong with Carrie's desire; in fact, it is part of our God-given design. Simply put, we were designed for love.

The first truth we must realize is that it was God's original design for man and woman to be in a relationship with Him, and in this relationship all our needs for security, confidence, and unconditional love are met. As we discussed, because of sin's entrance into the world, we are born into a broken world where we are separated from our God. This is the root cause of our insecurity and search for love today.

But God also designed us to be in relationships with one another. Right from the start, after creating the first man, Adam, God said, "It is not good for man to be alone" (Gen. 2:18). So as part of the original design, God created for him Eve, the first woman. As we saw in the beginning, when God, the Ultimate Matchmaker, set up these two lovebirds, the Bible says "they became one flesh." The oneness, the unity, the togetherness, and the intimacy we desire in relationships are all part of God's original design for us. His perfect plan is for two individuals to become one, and He calls this relationship marriage.

The oneness, the unity, the togetherness, and the intimacy we desire in relationships are all part of God's original design for us.

But as we know, sin entered the world and destroyed not only the harmony of Adam and Eve's relationship with God but also this harmony with one another. It is the loss of the primary relationship with God that causes all of our insecurity and unrest today. So, while our desires for human relationships are good, the desires can be disastrous when we attempt to stuff the holes in our hearts with persons. Those persons, no matter how wonderful, will always be a misfit for the God-shaped hole. Only God can fill the God-spot. And until we allow Him to do so, we will continue to leak insecurity, anxieties, and pain.

Our purest form of self becomes an intoxicated essence that reeks of habitual mistakes and continual longings.

The God-spot is easy to recognize: the empty ache in our souls that never seems to be satisfied. Because we are created by God and for God, the primary relationship our hearts are designed for is one with Him. But so often, when we feel discontent or incomplete, we think the solution to our problem is in meeting The One. We often tell ourselves, "If only I could find Mr. Right, then I would be satisfied." So often, we mistake our hearts' longing for God and His unfailing love as a longing for romantic relationships.

The girls of *Sex and the City* are no different from the rest of us; they, too, have a deep thirst that only God can quench. They crave real love. But their thirst can't be quenched by Cosmos, and their cravings can't be satisfied by cupcakes. They long to feel acceptance and to know the security of unconditional love. But, what they don't know is *what* this real love is and *where* it is ultimately found. As we all eventually find out, Cosmos and cupcakes, martinis and men, will leave us hung over, overweight, and undermined. Our purest form of self becomes an intoxicated essence that reeks of habitual mistakes and continual longings. Unfulfilled desires perpetrate exhausting journeys into emptiness. Empty glasses, empty arms, empty hearts. Can real love be the cure for this lonely addiction?

Let's find out. First of all, let's examine the elements of the prescription. What is "real love"? If we are all looking for it, what exactly is it? Can it even be defined? I would argue first of all that real love is more than a feeling. Feelings are fickle; they come and they go. Sure, there is an element of love that is emotional, but there is a deeper element—the one in which a choice is made, and that choice is to seek the best for the other individual, day in and day out.

When Carrie confesses to The Russian her desire for real love, she is describing romantic love. And this evokes images of passionate kisses, grand gestures of romance, and intense drama. (Ecstasy, girls!)

I'll give it to Carrie; there's not a drug out there that can compare with the feeling of romantic love. The chemistry, the attraction, the longing to be near the other person—it is thrilling. But here's the catch: there comes a day in every romance when the buzz wears off. Endorphins stabilize, rational thinking returns, and the bliss of romantic love turns into grocery shopping, paying bills, and changing diapers.

Our culture exalts romantic love to a godlike status—like a god in the sense that many women place their highest hopes for life and fulfillment in a person. Women hope for completion in something that was never designed to complete them. Everything in our culture sends this message: music, movies, poetry, even notes passed in high school— we are conditioned to believe that *if* we find Mr. Right, then all of our problems will go away. And the reality of the situation is this: we are all busting our butts to find our soul mates—these ideal men who we believe will remedy the aches in our souls. But girls, our souls don't need mates. Our souls need their Maker.

> *Girls, our souls don't need mates. Our souls need their Maker.*

Whew. Heavy sigh. OK, back to our question. Do we have a faulty image of love that is setting us up for disappointment and disillusionment? If we define love simply as an emotion, that definition sets us up for failure in a long-term relationship like marriage because emotional fragile love will fail when the hormones stabilize and we find ourselves staring back at an imperfect person. I would argue that the love Carrie is searching for is great, but it doesn't satisfy the soul's thirst for very long. The love she describes is blissful but fleeting, and it ultimately doesn't fill the soul. To place our hope for completion and fulfillment in a romantic relationship/ person will leave us empty time and time again.

Disappointment

Searching for a soul-filling, unconditional, perfect love in anyone other than God Himself will leave us disappointed and disillusioned. The search itself is destructive because in the end we find that no one can fill our emptiness or give us the security that comes from God alone. But in our society, every romantic movie and fairy tale teaches us to place our hope for this love in a person. We buy into the notion that Prince Charming will sweep us off of our feet and we will never again deal with the wicked stepmother of emptiness or the evil queen of insecurities. As a result, we believe the myth that the perfect persons, our soul mates, will be the ones who can complete us and meet all our needs.

As a single woman I am not immune to the desire for love, nor am I free from the longing for a marriage relationship. But I've come to realize single girls can fall prey to the grass-is-greener mentality by thinking, *If only I were married, then I wouldn't feel lonely or empty inside.* Little do we know how far from the truth this thought really is. Recently, I've had a whole slew of my married friends confess to me that some of their loneliest days have been as married women. Their husbands are wonderful but inadequate at filling their souls. The simple truth is, marriage doesn't make you happy; it just makes you married.

Like Charlotte, I'm a single woman. I have an incredible life. I have the best friends any woman could ever dream of. I've been blessed by God to travel the world. And all my essential needs are met: food, shelter, transportation, clothing, shoes (sandals, stilettos, running, flats, kitten heels, platforms, wedges), boots (flats, heels, cowboy, tall, ankle, scrunch, riding), and handbags. But, despite all of these blessings, I would be lying to you if I didn't confess there is something I don't have that I truly desire. I don't have a husband. When I plan my calendar and think of the future, it's just me. Holidays, hurricanes, couples events, tax forms, automobile problems, birthday parties, and the list could go on. There are times the desire is so real it is palpable. The desire can at times turn to pain, but through it all I've learned the secret of contentment.

The simple truth is, marriage doesn't make you happy; it just makes you married.

As a single girl, there are two truths that I must hold in balance in order to be content. First, God created me for relationship, so my desire for a husband is not wrong; it is good. Second, even though I was designed to be in relationship, my ultimate contentment, satisfaction, and happiness will never be achieved simply through a human relationship. I was designed for something far bigger, far greater, something far more satisfying.

Thirsty Girl Meets Jesus

It cracks me up how some people think the Bible is totally irrelevant to our modern culture. This makes me laugh because clearly these critics haven't opened a copy of God's Word lately. For instance, in the Bible is the story of a woman who, like many of us, found herself "looking for love in all the wrong places." She, too, hoped the deep thirst of her soul would be quenched in a relationship with a man.

Her story is found in the book of John, chapter 4, and she is often referred to as "the woman at the well." Let me start by giving you a little background info that will help you appreciate the power of this woman's story. Typically, women in that culture went to a well to get water for their families early in the morning or late in the evening, when the weather was cooler and transporting the heavy water jar would be easier (side note: Paris Hilton, if you are reading this, a well is where people would go to get water before the days of indoor plumbing). But this woman went at midday, right at the peak of the heat. Why the weird schedule? Well . . . let's just say she didn't really fit in with the other ladies.

Imagine *Desperate Housewives* set in Israel about two thousand years ago. She was the girl on the block whom all the other women despised. She was known as the town tramp. It was emotionally painful for her to go to the well at the normal time of day because she knew she would hear the critical comments and see the disdain in the eyes of the other women. Her love life, or lust life, had been fodder for the village gossips for years, so she chose to avoid the whole situation. So at noon she lugged her empty water jar to the well—alone. And it was in this moment that this broken, disappointed-with-life, and empty-as-her-water-jar woman had a life-changing encounter with Jesus Christ. For the empty water jar was the perfect symbol for her life. I guess you could call it a divine appointment.

> *He [Jesus] came to a town of Samaria. . . .*
> *Jacob's well was there, and Jesus, worn out from*
> *His journey, sat down at the well. . . . A woman*
> *of Samaria came to draw water. "Give Me a*
> *drink," Jesus said to her.* John 4:5–7

Now, just as strange as it was for this woman to be at the well at noon, it was even stranger still that Jesus purposely went out of His way to meet her. Major cultural taboos were being crossed here. First, Jesus was a Jewish man, and in that day Jews did not associate or speak to people from her region, which was called Samaria. It would be the modern-day equivalent of the racial tension that existed in the southern part of the United States between blacks and whites in the 1960s. But Jesus doesn't judge a person by her race. Jesus looks past the externals of a person and speaks straight to the issues of the heart. The second cultural taboo broken that day was a gender one. It was not acceptable in that culture for men to speak to women in public. So, you can understand why this woman was doubly surprised when this Jewish man spoke to her.

> *"How is it that You, a Jew, ask for a drink from me, a Samaritan woman?" she asked Him. For Jews do not associate with Samaritans.*
> *Jesus answered, "If you knew the gift of God, and who is saying to you, 'Give Me a drink,' you would ask Him, and He would give you living water."*   John 4:9–10

Imagine this scene: Jesus, weary from traveling the hot dusty roads of Israel, sat down by a well and began a conversation with a woman by simply asking her for a drink. Her response was curt and defensive. She reminded Jesus that she was not only a woman but a Samaritan woman. Who did He think He was to speak to her? Jesus, not dissuaded by her defensiveness, ignored her sharp tongue and turned the conversation to the real issue: her thirst, not His. You see, this woman's secret thirst was the real reason for this divine encounter.

> *"Sir," said the woman, "You don't even have a bucket, and the well is deep. So where do you get this 'living water'?"* John 4:11

Clearly she was confused. How could this Jewish man give her a drink? He was obviously empty handed. But Jesus led the discussion, and He turned the conversation from one about physical thirst to the real problem: her soul's thirst for "real love" and His ability to quench it forever.

> *Jesus said, "Everyone who drinks from this water will get thirsty again. But whoever drinks from the water that I will give him will never get thirsty again—ever! In fact, the water I will give him will become a well of water springing up within him for eternal life."*
> *"Sir," the woman said to Him, "give me this water so I won't get thirsty and come here to draw water."* John 4:13–15

Obviously, girlfriend hadn't clued in yet. She definitely was interested in this mysterious water Jesus offered, but she still didn't realize He was diagnosing her spiritual problem of "looking for love in all the wrong places."

> *"Go call your husband," He told her, "and*
> *come back here."*
> *"I don't have a husband," she answered.*
> *"You have correctly said, 'I don't have a*
> *husband,'" Jesus said. "For you've had five hus-*
> *bands, and the man you now have is not your*
> *husband. What you have said is true."*
>
> John 4:16–18

Five husbands? What happened? My mind reels with questions. I try to imagine this woman's journey from marriage to marriage, each time with a glimmer of hope that perhaps this time she would finally find the love her soul craved. My heart breaks for the disappointment I know she must have felt and the sheer disillusionment that settled in after a while. I wonder if she shacked up with the last guy because she'd given up hope of finding real love altogether—and just simply settled for the life she was living. Here's the thing I love about Jesus: He went looking for the girl who was losing hope, throwing in the towel, and in desperate need of a soul-satisfying love. I know because He came looking for me.

Notice what Jesus did in this conversation: He used the issue of the woman's physical thirst to expose her true need. Jesus asked her to go get her husband in order to reveal the real problem: the fact that she had searched from man to man to find satisfaction for her soul, and yet she was still empty. Husband number one didn't satisfy; maybe number two would do the trick. On and on she went until she was living with someone who was not even her husband. She'd reached a dead-end street in her journey of looking for love.

While living together may be accepted by many in our culture, it certainly wasn't in that day and time. Jesus didn't point out her marital history to shame or condemn her; He pointed out her looking-for-love problem so that she could finally find what she was looking for in Him. He told her, "Everyone who drinks of this water will be thirsty again, but whoever drinks the water I give him will never thirst. Indeed, the water I give him will become in him a spring of water welling up to eternal life."

Water is a great symbol for God because without water the body will shut down and our internal organs will collapse. The same is true of a life separated from God. Physically, we can't survive without water—and we can't *really live* without Jesus. Friend, do you feel shut down? Does your heart feel as if it might collapse? Read on.

Jesus Christ, the Son of God, came to satisfy the deep thirst of our souls. The definition of *thirst* is "to painfully feel the want and to eagerly long for something." Scripture is filled with imagery of God being compared to water for man's thirsty soul. For example, Psalm 42:1–2 reads, "As the deer pants for streams of water, so my soul pants for you, O God. My soul thirsts for God, for the living God" (NIV). So what are you waiting for, girls? Come on, drink up!!!

My Best Friend's Wedding

Here is the true story of a girl who drank before her wedding. She drank to calm her nerves. She drank to have giddy joy. She drank to find courage. She drank to have confidence in her decision. And she drank to quench her thirst *before* she walked down the aisle. Her drink of choice? Living Water. A true, two-hundred-proof dose of Jesus Christ, the lover of her soul. She is my best friend, and she recently married. I can still call her my best friend because she didn't make me wear some awful bridesmaid dress or endure the single woman's humiliation, the dreaded bouquet toss. (Disclaimer: I apologize to the bride who still loves a good bouquet toss. But after being in a gazillion weddings, I'm a little over it. It's nothing personal. I'm sure your wedding will be lovely.)

As the music played and the sanctuary doors opened for the wedding processional, I walked down the aisle as a bridesmaid rejoicing over the fact that my dear friend was marrying an incredible man who loves her dearly. As I stood by her side as a witness to their marriage vows, I was reminded of this chapter, and I realized I was an eyewitness to God's design. You see, before me stood two people very much in love. (The kind of mushy, please-don't-make-me-gag kind of love that can make you sick to be around sometimes.) But more than just romantic love, these two know *real* love. Sacrificial, self-giving, lay-your-life-down kind of love. These are two individuals who made a decision to walk through life together, through sickness and health, poverty and wealth, good times and bad—until death do them part. And they meant every word of it.

It is an amazing commitment if you stop to think about it. But the thing I loved about this wedding is that I know that both of them as individuals found the ultimate love their hearts hungered for in Jesus Christ long before they met each other. They didn't come together as incomplete halves hoping the other would somehow make them feel whole. They aren't parasites trying to suck life out of someone else. They aren't looking to the other person to make them complete. Their hearts were secure before they ever met the other. It was a beautiful moment. It is a picture of what God intends.

I have the privilege of witnessing many marriages like this one—marriages that are well past the honeymoon stage; ones that have endured infertility, economic crisis, family turmoil, and emotional breakdowns, and today they are still thriving and strong. These marriages are built on a firm foundation of love and trust. But once again, what I see as the common thread in each of these amazing unions is individuals who first allow God to fill their hearts with His love and who as individuals find their security in a relationship with Him. While their partners bring richness and joy, they are not the source of ultimate satisfaction. That job belongs to God alone; therefore, they don't live in disappointment or disillusionment because of an expectation that their mates will meet their every need and desire—they are free to love the other because their hearts have first been filled by God's love. Take my advice: do something for yourself today. Have that drink your heart is craving.

chapter four

Looking for Love in Approval

Are there some women put in the world just to make you feel bad about yourself?
CARRIE BRADSHAW OF *SEX AND THE CITY*
Season 3, episode 33, "Attack of the 5'10" Woman"

t was supposed to be research. Just research. But as I watched this particular episode of *Sex and the City* I felt like my own private struggles paraded before me on the television screen. I shifted in my chair, dropped my pen, stared back at the TV, and surrendered to the pain—allowing hot tears to flow down my cheeks. Carrie's tears triggered my own. Had the writers of *Sex and the City* secretly read my journal? Did they know the pain I was experiencing? I suppose the answer is yes. Yes, simply because my pain is a pain most women know all too well—the pain of a broken heart.

Sex and the City is so popular among women because the experiences, longings, and frustrations of the characters reflect the real-life struggles and insecurities that we, the real women on the other side of the television screen, know all too well. Granted, most of us can't afford designer shoes or fathom the glamorous lifestyle, but the hearts of women are the same—it doesn't matter if our hearts are clothed in Gucci or the Gap.

Carrie Bradshaw's off-and-on-again relationship with Mr. Big is the driving plotline of *Sex and the City*. The anguish and turmoil she experiences in this relationship is what keeps many women coming back each week for more. In the episode "Attack of the 5'10" Woman," Carrie comes face-to-face with a painful reality, and this reality is one that most women have experienced. But what most women don't know is *the rest of the story*.

The Wedding Section

It is a lovely Sunday in Manhattan as Samantha, Miranda, Charlotte, and Carrie enjoy brunch at a local café. Coffee, home fries, and girlfriends—for the girls of *Sex and the City,* this is the ideal morning. Today, their girl talk is centered on what Carrie describes as "the single woman's sports page—the *New York Times* wedding section." I'll be honest, when Carrie compared the wedding section to a sports page, I laughed out loud. I've found myself on many occasions fumbling through the various advertisements and editorials of a hefty Sunday paper in order to find the truly important section—and to satisfy some deep female curiosity.

Just as men read the sports page to find out scores and stats, women turn to the wedding section to do the very same thing—except the stats we are checking aren't batting averages or football rankings. We keep track of *far* more important issues, such as: Who's engaged? Who wore Vera Wang? *How many* bridesmaids did she have? Where did they go on their honeymoon? Not to mention one of my favorite reasons for reading this section is discovering the couple's "back story." Where did they go to college? How did they meet? How did he propose? But sometimes, if I'm honest, reading the wedding section evokes something else; it can stir in my heart the question, *What about me?* I'm pretty sure I'm not the only girl who has ever felt this way.

Charlotte entertains and simultaneously tortures the group at breakfast this particular morning by reading aloud engagement stories. Each of the women takes turns criticizing the couples mentioned, which causes Carrie to make an astute observation:

> *It's amazing how upset we can get about the marital status of strangers.*
>
> Season 3, episode 33, "Attack of the 5'10" Woman"

Don't you love how Carrie can flat-out say what most of us are secretly thinking? Why *is it* we get so upset about the marital status of other women? Why do we get jealous when another girl gets the three-carat, Tiffany-set diamond ring? Why does it dig into our hearts when we hear someone else's engagement story? I think we all know the reason we feel this way. Frankly, each wedding invitation we receive in the mail not only includes a map to the reception and a response card, but it also comes loaded for some of us with *the question:* why not me?

The "Big" Rejection

As Charlotte flips the newspaper page, she discovers a familiar face, something she wishes she could hide—Mr. Big and Natasha's wedding announcement. You see, Big is Carrie's ex-boyfriend and the love she has yet to get over. She knew he was engaged, yet seeing their full-page announcement in the *New York Times* stirs up a whole host of insecurities and questions in Carrie's heart.

Breakups are brutal agony. As only a good girlfriend can do, Charlotte reads the article describing Big's wedding and sits with Carrie as she cries through her pain. But here's my question: Why is Carrie hurting? What's the source of her pain? Is there something deeper here than simply missing Big or just being sad about the loss of their relationship? The sad truth is this: Carrie is experiencing the excruciating pain of rejection.

Can you relate to her agony? I know I can. Most of us have gone through the pain of a breakup and know all too well the wave of emotions that are flooding Carrie's heart. As I watched this episode, I wanted to step into the scene, a pint of double fudge ice cream in hand, and hold her hand as she cried. For Carrie, the fact that Big married someone else sends a taunting message to her heart that says, *You're not good enough.*

Rejection is something most of us have experienced in some form or another. It could be as simple as not getting picked for the school sports team, not making cheerleader, or not getting asked to your high-school prom. Or perhaps you spent a lifetime not being accepted because of your looks, race, economic status, or intellect. Or maybe you worked hard for something only to receive the dreaded letter of rejection. For some, the pain of rejection is even more severe and is rooted in a deep childhood wounding such as divorce, abandonment, abuse, or neglect. Whatever the degree, many women walk away from these life experiences thinking, *Who I am is simply not good enough.*

In this episode, after reading the wedding announcement describing Natasha's life, family, and career, Carrie compares herself with Natasha and in turn questions her own value. Her feelings of rejection cause her to measure her own worth by Natasha, and now she feels not only rejected but also insignificant and unlovable. While Carrie's hurt is understandable, her solution to her pain causes even more problems.

Approval Junkie

Carrie's insecurity and inner drive for approval are revealed when later that week she devises a way to see Natasha while "looking fabulous."

Don't miss Carrie's motivation. She wants to *prove* she is amazing. She is obsessed with gaining Natasha's approval and with proving that she is the better woman. The feelings of insecurity and rejection drive Carrie to go to great lengths to earn the approval she craves. For starters, Carrie, fixated on her appearance, goes into huge debt to buy the perfect outfit for her encounter with Natasha. Carrie believes, as many women do, that if she feels more beautiful or more stylish, then her insecurity will go away.

This is a great commentary on how many women live their lives every day. Insecure and fearing rejection, they strive, perform, and conform who they are in hopes of finding acceptance. Some of us will do anything to feel that we belong. Literally, we become approval junkies, performing and transforming into whoever or whatever we think will give us that stamp of approval. Ultimately, we are looking to others to tell us who we are. The consequence of this thought pattern is living on a constant roller coaster of emotions, dependent on the fickle appraisal of men to tell us our worth. This is just another example of how we are looking for love in all the wrong places.

I love coffee. Now, I know it is the drink of choice for most Americans these days, but I've been a coffee addict long before Starbucks landed on every street corner. I love the aroma and the taste, but I also love how a cup of joe can be the perfect companion to a long chat with a good friend. Each morning I stumble into my kitchen in a daze and fumble with a high-tech machine that makes the best coffee ever! I love the stuff.

Like an addict craving the next fix, I lived for other people's opinions. I didn't just want other people to accept me; I needed their stamp of approval and would constantly conform and transform to earn their acceptance.

I must confess, there's been another addiction in my past: I, too, am a recovering approval junkie. Like an addict craving the next fix, I lived for other people's opinions. I didn't just want other people to accept me; I *needed* their stamp of approval and would constantly conform and transform to earn their acceptance. As with any addiction, there are serious side effects. Approval junkies look to another person to define their value. The downside to finding our worth from others' approval is that we allow people to label us, defining who we are and what we are worth. Let me give you a few examples from my own life.

The Labels

She walked through the crowd of intimidated ninth-grade students with an attitude that spoke of the power she held. Her approval or disapproval meant the future of your high-school popularity status. In a matter of minutes, she sized up the new crop that would be under her command and systematically gave us each a label: "in" or "out." The agenda for the evening was to initiate the freshmen who would belong to the popular crowd, but first, a major decision had to be made: who's cool? I guess you know by now where this is going. As the most popular girl in the high school looked my way, I could see the appraisal in her eyes long before the words ever left her lips. I was out. I didn't have a lot of money, so my clothes weren't the latest fashion trends. To make matters worse, I was still adjusting to the seven inches I'd grown in the past year. I guess you could say I was a little awkward. The only person who thought I was pretty was my mother.

That night I took on the label "uncool," and the rest of my high-school career was an effort to overcome that title. I desperately wanted to fit in, to be accepted, and to find approval in the eyes of my peers. This desire ultimately led me to conform my values and my personality many times over in hopes of gaining the coveted cool status. But this was only one of many labels that I acquired in life. A few years before the high-school incident, I received a different label, one that I believed about myself for many, many years.

One bright, sunny day, a few weeks after my thirteenth birthday, I sat in my usual spot and waited for my mom to pick me up from school. Having time to kill, I chatted with the other students who had gathered to wait for their rides. If you've ever watched the Discovery Channel, you've probably seen a similar incident to the one I am about to describe—except on this occasion, the prey about to be devoured was not a baby elephant stalked by a pride of lions; the prey of the moment was me. The smell of fresh blood was in the air. Let's face it; thirteen-year-old girls can be vicious.

On this particular day the object of ridicule was my hair. You see, I had curly hair long before Carrie Bradshaw made it fashionable. And to add insult to injury, I was blessed with this hair before anyone formulated these fabulous new products for managing curl. So basically, instead of having a head of luscious waves, on most days I had a head of frizz. And please understand, not the "I just left the beach" kind of mess;

I'm talking about the real deal. I guess you would say I was an easy target.

The predator, a girl with perfectly coifed hair (and she knew it) approached me as her posse watched on and asked, "Do you wash your hair with *Mop & Glo* [a cleaning product for floors in the '80s]?" Laughter erupted around me. Tears welled up in my eyes as I realized she told me and everyone within hearing distance that my hair looked like a mop. I was so humiliated. It wasn't that I thought I was beautiful or anything, but at that moment I allowed someone else to put on me another label, and this time it read, "Hi, my name is Ugly."

The more you love someone, the more painful the rejection.

It would take years before I would be able to accept my appearance—and even longer before I made peace with public enemy number one: my hair. I fought it at every turn. Color, straightening irons, shag cut, razor cut, the Rachel cut, highlights, bangs, no bangs, long layers, velcro rollers, hot rollers, hot sticks, and, yes, I hate to admit it, the spiral perm. Each and every morning, I looked into the mirror and despised my own reflection. I didn't measure up. My hair didn't give me the approval I wanted, so I fought a daily battle to tame the mane and to hopefully transform myself into someone who would be accepted—if not accepted, then at least not publicly ridiculed.

The more you love someone, the more painful the rejection. Being rejected by someone close—a family member, boyfriend, spouse, or lifelong friend—can inflict deep emotional scars. As I reflect on this idea of labels, I know the most devastating label I took on in my life is one that read "unlovable." Painful experiences from my childhood coupled with a pretty significant heartbreak in college left me believing a fundamental lie about my identity: "You are unlovable."

Ugly. Uncool. Unlovable. I could add more labels to this list, but I think you get the picture. I lived much of my life by these definitions. As other painful events occurred in life (breakups, weight gain, acne, failure), I allowed these events to confirm the self-perception that was already established in my early years.

Something to Prove

Looking back, I can see how my heart, the core of who God created me to be, wanted to overcome these labels. I didn't want to settle for these definitions. The sum total of these messages left me with an identity of rejection: I am not accepted. I am not worthy of love. So my response was to strive, fight, perform, conform, manipulate, and do anything and everything to replace the feelings of rejection and shame I felt. I desired a love that would fill my emptiness and make me feel wanted, loved, and cherished.

The sad reality is that I am not alone. Many women go through life trying to overcome a label that was placed on them. What labels have you been given?

- Did a parent walk out and leave you feeling "unwanted"?
- Did a relationship end and cause you to believe that you, too, are "unlovable"?
- Have life experiences and people's opinions defined you in a way that still causes pain today?

If you're honest with yourself, you know you're still fighting to overcome it. Perhaps you feel labeled "unimportant" or "unnoticed." Why? Are you weighed down by the fear of rejection?

The fear of rejection is an incredible motivator. I believe it might be one of the most powerful influencers on the planet. Remember Carrie's Natasha-specific obsession? It was rooted in the fear of rejection. Think about it. What things do we do so that others will approve of us? What lengths do we go to in order to feel like we belong? How much money do we spend? How much time do we invest? How much of our daily effort is fueled by the desire to find acceptance? It's called "keeping up with the Joneses" for a reason. It's all about keeping up, measuring up, and beating the next girl. But why? What's the prize? If I win (i.e., by feeling prettier, smarter, sexier, richer, tanner . . .

than the next girl), does that mean I will finally feel loved for who I am? At what point do we really feel accepted?

Feelings of rejection are common to many women. It can be a subtle nagging that says, "You are not good enough," or it can be a full-blown assault on your identity that says, "You are worthless." These thoughts and feelings can be traced back to painful experiences, but ultimately they find their source in our separation from God. Let me explain.

Our souls' desperate need for the unconditional love that only God can give has left us both empty and searching for something or someone to fill the void. Separation from our Creator has also left us with nagging doubts and insecurities about our value and worth.

Remember, before sin entered the world, humanity didn't know the meaning of insecurity. We didn't experience the sting of rejection because there was only One who defined our value and worth. It was God Himself, living in the presence of His perfect love, who made us know at the core of our being that we are accepted. Outside of relationship with Him, we are like a ship lost at sea. Who am I? What's my value? Am I good? We have these questions, but now, instead of looking to God to define us, we turn to others, hoping their validation will fill the emptiness in our souls.

A tragic consequence of our separation from God is the treadmill of constant striving and performing to find love and acceptance. Our hearts are looking for love, the unconditional love of God, in the approval of people. Looking for love in approval is not exclusively a female issue; men struggle with this too. But I want to address two fundamental ways that we, as women, try to fill our God-spot with approval. The first is the appearance factor, and the second is the performance factor.

> *I'm a thirty-four-year-old woman with braces,*
> *and I'm on a liquid diet. Pain doesn't begin to*
> *cover it.* Miranda Hobbs of Sex and the City

The Appearance Factor

Mirror, mirror on the wall, who is the fairest of them all? Women learn from an early age that it pays to be pretty. The prettiest princess always rides away with the prince. Did you ever see the ugly stepsister win the guy? I don't think so. Then, from the time we hit puberty, the boys let us know just exactly what they think of a girl's appearance by ranking everything from her face to her body. And let's not forget the magazines: *Teen Vogue*, *YM*, *Seventeen*, and then the more mature publications, *Glamour*, *Cosmopolitan*, and *Allure* . . . all shouting the same thing—how you look matters.

Just today I was listening to some high-school girls play the game *Would You Rather?* The question of the moment was "Would you rather be obese and not able to lose weight or super thin—yet ugly?" The point of the game is the turmoil of the decision. Choose an ugly existence or a fat existence. Either choice is horrific to their young minds. Why? Because they've bought the lie that a woman's value is in her appearance.

Perhaps this is why the business of beauty is a billion-dollar industry. I'm embarrassed to admit how much money I spend on cosmetics. Marketers bombard us with advertisements promising everything from the fountain of youth in a bottle to a complete transformation in a pill. And aren't we suckers? My bathroom cabinets are filled with purchases that either didn't live up to the claim or simply didn't solve the main problem—an empty soul.

Beauty is a fickle business. What's in? What's hot? What is the current measure of beauty? It is an ever-changing target that we spend time, money, and energy primping to attain. Here's the bottom line. When I seek approval by my appearance, I place my self-worth at the mercy of another—leaving my emotional state and sense of value to be determined by a mere mortal. Who is the person in your life whose opinion can rock your world? Why do we give another person this much power?

Before we answer that question, let's think about the appearance factor. Achieving physical beauty and the obsession with looking younger have captured us. Television shows such as *Dr. 90210* and the former *Extreme Makeover* tout the benefits of cosmetic surgery. Typically, the one receiving the makeover states that boosting their self-esteem is the number-one reason for participating. Many who are chosen for these shows don't feel worthy of love or accepted because of their physical appearance, and they believe going under the knife is the solution to their problem. I often watch these programs and wonder what happened when the cameras stopped rolling. Was the insecurity still there long after the surgical scars had faded? Are there some things even the most skilled surgeon can't correct?

> *"I can be having a great day and see a picture of Christy Turlington and feel awful about myself."*
> —Charlotte,
> *Sex and the City*

While the desire to be beautiful itself is not wrong, there is a sinister side; it occurs when a woman finds her identity in her appearance. Many women wake up every morning to Judge Beauty. We look into the mirror and critique everything we see—frizzy hair, pale skin, cellulite, or whatever else the latest magazine shows us is wrong with our appearance. We compare ourselves to the images we see on television or to other women we see on the street and, as a result, feel depressed. As the *Sex and the City* character Charlotte once remarked, "I can be having a great day and see a picture of Christy Turlington and feel awful about myself."

Like Charlotte, most of us don't always like what we see looking back in the mirror. This leads us to all kinds of crazy activities. The desire for perfection in our appearances can be the root cause of self-hatred, depression, eating disorders, jealousy among friends, avoidance of social situations, and even financial debt procured in an effort to achieve *the look*. This begs the question, when is it enough? Because beauty is something that cannot be defined and is "in the eye of the beholder," who is it that determines how each person should look? I doubt most of us have ever seriously considered this question.

Can I tell you a secret? I am scared to death of the sales people at cosmetic counters. I'm not sure if it is the black cape they wear that reminds me of Darth Vader or if it's the fact that I can feel their scrutiny as soon as I walk through the department store doors. I get totally intimidated when they look at my skin and make that disapproving noise whenever I tell them I can't afford their expensive eye cream. Many times I've walked away, eye cream in hand, simply because I wanted the approval of the person behind the counter. Why do I give these people so much power?

We place ourselves at the mercy of ever-changing standards of beauty and constantly try to keep up with fashion trends, hairstyles, and body types—all fast-moving targets. Therefore, for us to seek love by our appearance is to constantly ride the roller coaster of public opinion and to never feel like we reached our destination. Can we ever rest knowing we are loved and accepted simply for who we are—without the frills of fashion and the covering of makeup?

Can we ever rest knowing we are loved and accepted simply for who we are—without the frills of fashion and the covering of makeup?

I'm amazed at how easy it is to fall into this trap. Each month when the *In Style* magazine arrives in my mailbox, I sit down and devour it from cover to cover. Immediately, I feel dissatisfied with my wardrobe because the editors have educated me on what I must buy in order to be *in*. It doesn't matter that I just managed to find a pair of boot cut jeans that I love; the fashion police are now telling me that I must revert to the skinny leg jean if I want to be cool. Too bad that the skinny leg jean makes my rear end look like an eighteen-wheeler flattened it out—but that doesn't seem to matter because skinny is the new thing. So bye-bye, boot cut. Have you ever wondered where the phrase "a slave to fashion" came from?

Flipping through these magazines also conjures

up other thoughts. I hate my eyebrows. If only I had green eyes. Why is my nose so big? I wish my skin looked like Heidi Klum's—and on and on the negative voice drones. My own Judge Beauty begins to criticize by pointing out zits, gray hair, and every other way I simply don't measure up. Every morning is a choice: to listen to the voice or not.

Finding approval from our appearance simply leaves us with either a self-deprecating loathing or an overinflated ego.

There is a serious danger when we measure our worth by our appearances. The consequences can swing from self-hatred to self-centeredness. Self-hatred can occur if we never achieve the perfect look and listen to the condemning voice that says "you are not good enough" if we don't meet some ever-changing standard of beauty. Looking for love in our appearance can also lead to an extreme form of self-centeredness, which results from a life that is focused only upon gaining approval by looking good. Therefore, our time, money, and thoughts are centered on achieving the goal. That doesn't leave much time to care for other people or their needs. Finding approval from our appearance simply leaves us with either a self-deprecating loathing or an overinflated ego.

This brand of looking for love should be called "the survival of the prettiest." Insecure and fearing rejection, many women turn on other women when they feel their source of esteem is threatened. One would hope we had outgrown this cattiness in high school, but the sad reality is that many women who seek approval through their appearance will consequently be competitive with other women throughout life.

I have one question: Does this work? Are we ever pretty enough, fashionable enough, or thin enough to fill the emptiness in our souls? You can call me Miss Obvious USA, but I think the answer is no. But, can our souls be filled with a love that drives away insecurities and the nagging self-doubts? The answer is yes! But before we get there, let's consider the other way we strive for approval.

The Performance Factor

Lights, camera, action! Some women live their entire lives on a virtual stage, performing for love. It's no wonder really. Performing for acceptance and approval—love—is ingrained in our culture. We are told as little kids, "Be good and you'll get a prize." Then later as we enter the academic arena, we find out that if we work hard in school we will be rewarded for our efforts. Somewhere along the way we get the message: work hard, perform well, and you will be rewarded. So it's logical why we would assume this performance-based system would work when it comes to finding the love and security our souls crave. But does it work? Can we ever gain enough accolades or earn enough credentials to erase the feelings of insecurity? Many of us try our hardest to overcome these feelings and wind up performing for love.

How do we perform for love? There is a multiplicity of ways. Some of us become people pleasers, constantly trying to keep the people around us happy—thinking that if we make others happy, then they will reward us with their acceptance. Likewise, we fear upsetting people because then they might not like us. Others focus on our careers, pouring our time and effort into our jobs because, secretly, this is where we find our value and worth. The thought pattern is as follows: *if* I am successful, *then* I am worthy of love.

I promise I don't live in front of the television. But there is yet another TV show that illustrates this truth. It is *VH1 Behind the Music.* There are many programs of this genre, and the gist is to portray the rise to fame of a celebrity, be that a musician, athlete, actor, or even those who are just famous for being famous.

There is a common formula to these biographies: achievement and emptiness. The musician typically begins by sharing his rise from obscurity and the passion for success that fueled his hard work. Normally the show will share photos of the icon as a kid singing at festivals, churches, or even *Star Search.* The majority of those interviewed had their hearts set on fame and fortune as kids.

The next stage of the program is what I like to call "hitting rock bottom." Here the celebrity tells of reaching his pinnacle of success and then, whenever he "has it all," coming to a point of sheer brokenness. Why? Because even after achieving all the accolades of success, he still hadn't found what he was looking for. All along the journey there has been this belief in the person's soul that said, *One day, when I finally achieve my goal, then I will be happy. One day, I will feel complete, if I . . . .* But the sad reality is this: no amount of money or worship of adoring fans can fill the emptiness of a soul. It is at this point that many turn to substances and spending to alleviate the disappointment they feel. And the next stop for most is rock bottom.

Behind the Music portrays on a large scale what most of us do on a small scale. We tell ourselves the same message: *One day, if I can do [fill in the blank] then I will be fulfilled. If I achieve this level of success, then I will be happy.* But more so, we tell ourselves that we need to prove our worth through these accomplishments.

It's easy to see why so many women today are on the verge. We are simply burned out and exhausted. We are driven to succeed not out of a desire to do a job with excellence but by the fear of failure—believing, if I'm not the top performer (highest GPA, top sales, employee of the month, etc.), then I am not valuable as a person. And just like our friend Carrie, we become obsessed with proving our worth.

We've been performing and doing to the point of collapse. The fear of rejection keeps many women working, striving, performing, conforming, and transforming over and over again. (I'm weary just thinking about it.) Our souls are starving for affirmation, and we will do anything to feed that hunger. This craziness is fueled by the fact that we've mixed up what we do with who we are. Most women today feel defined by a title or an occupation; therefore, that role is their source of esteem and worth. That being the case, the insecurity and incompleteness they feel on the inside drive them to get their props and affirmation from their particular role.

What Defines You?

This past spring I spoke on this topic to a group of women in my city. Prior to the talk I decided it would be a good idea if I did some research. So, I hit the streets with one agenda: to learn what real women believe gives them worth, value, and security. Armed with a video camera and a big smile, I walked up to complete strangers at my local Starbucks and asked women a simple question: "What defines you?"

Most of the women responded to my survey with an answer that said they felt defined by what they do:

wife, attorney, mom, student, therapist, sales, teacher, big sister, nurse, caregiver, and on the titles flowed. This small sampling of women left me with a question: do we women have intrinsic value simply for who we are, or is our value measured by what we do? Intrinsic value means to belong to something because of its very nature. If that is the case, then what is a person's value? And better yet, who is able to define that value?

I have some good news. Freedom is available— freedom from the insecurity and striving to find approval in our appearance and in our performance. For freedom to be real and lasting, a woman must know at the core of her being that she is accepted and that *who* she is, is absolutely good and lovable. To rid a woman's heart of insecurity, she must have real security. Not the kind of security that comes from a new outfit or the temporary praise of men but the kind that doesn't lose its sparkle— the kind that lasts. But where do this security and confidence come from? The real acceptance our hearts crave is uncovered in an encounter between Jesus and a girl like you and me, a girl who was looking for love in all the wrong places.

The Jesus Factor

The Bible tells a story of a woman who, like me and other women I know, was branded with a harsh label. She'd had a pretty rough life. I guess you could say she was a wild girl. Everyone in the village knew her or at least knew *of* her. She was labeled, and the names were not nice: slut, easy, crazy girl, desperate, used. Do you know a girl like her? Are you a girl like her?

This woman's particular label read "sinner." Everyone in her village called her by that name, and they didn't want to associate with a girl like her. She had a bad reputation. I imagine she had a pretty lonely existence. Who knows the full story behind her label? But one thing is for sure: she was ready to get rid of it.

One evening a prominent man in her town hosted a dinner party and invited Jesus to attend. Although the Scripture doesn't tell us all the details, we can infer that the sinful woman had some sort of encounter with Jesus prior to this event. We know this because once she learned that Jesus would dine at the man's home that evening, she broke all rules of etiquette and made her way there—uninvited, I might add. Her purpose in going was to simply be near Jesus. She intended to worship Him (Luke 7:37–39).

You might be asking, what's so special about Jesus? Good question. In Jesus Christ, this woman found the unconditional love and acceptance her heart had always hungered for; and, what's more, when she came to Him that day in adoration, He did something for her that would change her life forever: He removed her old label.

The sinful woman entered the dinner party and made a beeline for Jesus. The crowd of onlookers whispered. The host of the evening snickered, "If He is a real prophet, then He would know what 'sort' of woman she is . . . 'she is a sinner.'" Can you hear the judgment in the host's voice? Jesus, undeterred by the condemnation swirling about Him, turned to the woman and, in a word, removed the label she'd been carrying for years. Looking her in the eye, Jesus said, "Your sins are forgiven." One simple statement from Jesus, and her whole life was transformed. No longer was she called "sinner"; Jesus gave her a new name— "forgiven" (Luke 7:40–50).

As I imagine this scene, I think about the onlookers—the ones with the smug, self-satisfied expressions because they felt superior to the woman with the bad rep. I like to imagine their astonishment as Jesus gave her this new label. I'm sure they were a little ticked off. Their idea of religion was that you must work hard and perform perfectly in order to be accepted by God. How dare Jesus so easily wipe away this woman's sins? Who does He think He is?

I think my hunch is right because Scripture tells us that when Jesus did this they turned to one another and asked, "Who is this man who even forgives sins?" Basically, they all wanted to know one thing: what gave Jesus the right to change her label?

Who Is This Man?

This is one of my favorite questions in the entire Bible. Who is this man? People always marveled at Jesus. Sure, He did lots of things that made people scratch their heads in awe—such as multiplying food to feed the hungry, healing the paralyzed, turning water into wine so that a wedding wouldn't be a total flop, and other drop-your-jaw-in-awe miracles. But these things didn't get Jesus into trouble. What caused Him trouble with the religious authorities of the day was when He did things and said things that only God Himself was supposed to say and do. Such as, gee, I don't know . . . claim to be God. When Jesus went around doing stuff like that, well . . . that's precisely why the leaders of the day wanted to kill Him.

The situation with the woman at the dinner party was just one of those moments. When Jesus had the audacity to forgive her sins, He did something that everyone knew and fully understood could be done only by God Himself. That is why the people asked, "Who is this man who even forgives sins?"

Jesus has the authority to forgive our sins and change labels because He is God. This is the Christian message. God Himself stepped on earth to rescue us from sin and from all the ways we are looking for love apart from Him—our empty attempts to fill our God-spot.

The Bible clearly teaches that Jesus is God. In the New Testament book of Colossians, we are told that "by Him [Jesus] *all things* were created, both in the heavens and on earth, visible and invisible, whether thrones or powers or rulers or authorities—*all things* have been created through Him and for Him" (1:16 NASB). This passage is powerful. Jesus is the Creator of all things. If this is true, then that answers our question. Jesus has every right to change a label and to forgive sins because He is the Creator and Designer. It is His right to name His precious creation—you—whatever He pleases.

This was God's intent from the beginning. As we discussed, God's original design for humankind was to live in the presence of His perfect love and to know without a shadow of a doubt that we are loved and accepted. But then, with the entrance of sin into the world, we got separated from the only One who can authentically tell us who we are. That is when our thinking got all jacked up. After sin entered the world, we went looking for love (acceptance and affirmation) in all the crazy places that we've been discussing. And that's precisely why Jesus, who is God, came to earth. He came to set us free from the craziness.

From Rejected to Accepted

Reflecting on the transformation of this sinful woman, we see one last but crucial part of her story.

Acceptance. Here, this girl, a social reject, found unconditional acceptance from Jesus. When she approached Jesus, He accepted her. He didn't look at her with condemnation. He didn't scorn her. He didn't tell her to go and clean up her act before she approached Him. Jesus offered her something she'd never known before—grace. Grace is when we are given something we don't deserve. This means we didn't earn it—no performance necessary.

Like many women, she knew the pain of rejection. But God extended to her the very thing her heart had been searching for: acceptance. And try as I may to express it in words, there is nothing that compares to knowing you are loved. This knowledge brings rest to the soul. This acceptance tells our souls, "You don't need to *prove* anything."

I have a painting of the scene of the formerly sinful woman worshipping at the feet of Jesus. It is one of my dearest possessions. My best friends gave it to me as a gift because they know that her story is *my* story. This painting serves as a daily reminder of what Jesus has done in my life. His love and acceptance transformed my life and set me free from looking for love in all the wrong places. No longer do I need to live for the approval of people or to try to find my value in my appearance because the only One who is able and worthy of defining me has already spoken a word over me.

Jesus says to us in His Word: We are not rejected; we are accepted. We are not unlovable; we are His treasured creation. We are not unwanted; we are chosen. We are not forsaken; we are children of the King. And the more we know Jesus and allow Him to love us and to tell us *who* we are, the more the old labels fade away. The performance treadmill slows to a stop as we allow the One Voice that really matters to speak to us who we are.

"Big" Is Not God

In a relationship with Jesus Christ, women no longer have to live trying to prove their worth. Now, the God of the Universe, the One who rescues us, tells us definitively who we are. We no longer need to feel weighed down by the fear of rejection. There is a security that is offered to us from God Himself that sets us free from finding our worth in fickle things such as our appearance or performance or, even better, the approval of another person.

Perhaps this is why I feel so deeply for Carrie Bradshaw as I watch *Sex and the City*. Sure, I can relate to her pain, but more so, I hurt that she doesn't know that Big's rejection is not the final authority on who she is. When a guy walks out and breaks your heart, he doesn't have the right to label you unlovable or unwanted. His rejection does not have to define you.

Why? Because *your* "Mr. Big" is not God. Repeat after me: [*Fill in the blank with his name*] is not God.

When we give someone the power to define us, we put that person in the place of God. God alone has the right to define you—meaning, the only person who can tell you who you are is Jesus. Take it from a girl who searched high and low for someone to tell me who I am. And ladies, just let me say, Jesus says I am l-o-v-e-d! No more sticky labels for this girl. I know who I am because I know *Whose* I am.

> When we give someone the power to define us, we put that person in the place of God.

chapter five

Looking for Love in a Hook-up

Later that night I got to thinking about safe sex . . . .
When you crawl in bed with someone, is sex ever safe?
CARRIE BRADSHAW OF *SEX AND THE CITY*
Season 3, episode 41, "Running with Scissors"

There wasn't a dry eye in the place. Before me sat a room full of women, each burned from "looking for love in all the wrong places." Where had most of them looked for love? Sex. Yep, they'd all believed the lie . . . the Samantha Jones lie, that is.

To me, each girl was beautiful, successful, smart, and fun. Just minutes before my talk began, I overheard them chatting about fashion, hairstyles, upcoming parties, and, of course, men. One reminded me of an old friend and another of a sister. My point? This assembly of women could be found in any city in America: Seattle, L.A., Tampa, Kansas City, Dallas, and, yes, Manhattan.

They were the Carries, Samanthas, Charlottes, and Mirandas of my city. They were amazing women, but behind their fashionable clothes and successful careers were women hurting and disappointed with where their own journey of looking for love had taken them. Sure, some of these young, single women had boasted at one time or another of their sexual conquests. Bragging of the pleasure they had in hooking up, they tried to convince themselves and their girlfriends that they were happy in the land of sex without strings.

But as I shared my own story of the emotional devastation that occurred in my soul from sex outside of marriage, the façade of happiness began to crumble. Tears flowed down their cheeks, and I watched as their eyes reflected back to me the deep pain in their souls. Something I said struck a chord.

They still hadn't found what they were looking for.

It's all so confusing, isn't it? On television we watch women engage in premarital sex with numerous partners and walk away unscathed. Take *Friends*, for example. Who knows how many men Rachel slept with, and yet she always seemed perky and fun. Why is it so easy on TV? Everyone wakes up in the morning looking beautiful in the land of makeup artists. If an actor makes a mistake or misses a line, the director simply yells, "Cut!" and they reshoot the scene. And the editors (girls, who wouldn't love an editor?), they get to cut out the bland, boring, embarrassing, and just plain unwanted details. The editor makes it all seem so picture perfect.

Hollywood fuels a belief that sex outside of marriage is positive not negative. For the most part, the dramas, sitcoms, and movies we watch portray premarital sex as

In the real world, sex isn't "just sex."

the natural and expected progression in a relationship. On the television screen it all looks so easy. Your favorite character never has an STD. If by chance someone gets pregnant, she seems to effortlessly adjust to the challenges and demands of raising an infant. Sex is simple. Sex is "just sex," as Samantha Jones would say on *Sex and the City*.

Unlike Hollywood, real life has a way of being messy.

In the real world, sex isn't "just sex." Samantha is the sexual power player of the series. Bold and aggressive, she views sex as a means of power, pleasure, and personal glory. She relishes in her conquests to her girlfriends like a Wall Street broker bragging about a deal.

Of the four, she is the most sexually liberated, and most of her story lines revolve around the many men and sex she has. She is confident, strong, outspoken, and a self-proclaimed "try-sexual" (meaning she'll try anything once).

For Ms. Jones, sex is only an activity; it's a sport. Hooking up doesn't mean anything. She is one to boast proudly of her sexual conquests and devours men like a ten-year-old with candy. Samantha Jones alleges she is the future of women. Evolved past pesky emotions and that old-fashioned need for commitment, she claims to be free from any expectations from her sexual encounters.

But is she really free?

A quick survey of Samantha and her friends uncovers the truth. Carrie is frustrated and needy when Big won't commit to her after months of sex without strings. Miranda is defensive and angry toward men after years of feeling used and abandoned. Charlotte is ashamed when a man treats her as an object to be used and discarded. And Samantha, try as she may to deny it, is jealous—fiercely jealous—when the man she is sleeping with is busted sleeping with another woman. (It seems she does have expectations after all, doesn't she?)

The problem I have with *Sex and the City* is this: the girls never seem to wake up and learn from their mistakes. There is a reason Carrie is an emotional yo-yo when it comes to Mr. Big. There is a really good explanation as to why Miranda is defensive and doesn't trust men after years of casual sex. Charlotte has every reason to feel cheap and demeaned when she's treated like a whore. And Samantha, *hellooooooooo* . . . jealousy is a natural response when you catch the man your soul is bonded to in bed with another woman. All of these reactions are dead-on *and* completely normal. Every woman in their "Choos" would have the same symptoms. By now, friends, you can probably make the diagnosis yourself. Their disorder is simply a result of sex outside of God's design, sex outside of God's prescribed order.

However, in one episode of *Sex and the City*, it seems a light dawns, even if briefly, on Samantha concerning her attitude toward sex. This episode, "All or Nothing," reveals to Samantha that she just might not be the ideal future for women.

Does Samantha Jones Really Have It All?

Samantha Jones has arrived . . . or so she believes. In this particular episode, the four friends gather for food, drinks, laughter, and to toast their "fabulous lives." Samantha raises her glass and tells the others, "We have it all. Great friends. Good jobs and plenty of good sex" (season 3, episode 40, "All or Nothing").

Ironically, the next morning Samantha awakens to find out that she indeed does have it all: sniffling, sneezing, coughing, aching, stuffy head, fever (and no man as her medicine). Samantha has the flu. Sick, alone, and desperate for help, she opens her little black book and calls the many men in her life whom she sleeps with, hoping someone will come to her aid. Their responses are positive when they think she is calling for a hookup, but they are suddenly unavailable when they discover the real purpose of her call. She calls every man in her black book, and not one of her so-called lovers will come to her rescue. Miserable, she realizes that the men she's slept with want her for sex; but once they've used her, they aren't around when it really matters.

So, for the million-dollar question: does Samantha Jones *really* have it all?

This episode uncovers the reality that Samantha feels used and abandoned by the men with whom she has sex. Yet, the show offers no real hope or choice for Samantha other than to continue down the same empty path she's traveled thus far. It seems the writers want viewers to simply disregard her regret as a bad case of the flu. But Samantha's regret has nothing to do with a forty-eight-hour virus. The illness only illuminates the darkness of her situation. Instead of "having it all," Samantha Jones is left feeling lonely, ashamed, and empty.

Certainly, I'm not condemning Samantha or any woman like her—quite the opposite. I speak out because not only do I know this emptiness from experience, but I desire to see other women set free from it. I've witnessed firsthand the emotional and physical devastation that occurs in the lives of women who engage in sex outside of marriage. I've wiped tears from the eyes of a friend who carries the shame of a sexually transmitted disease. I've held the hands of girls who are frightened and disillusioned with the reality of an unplanned pregnancy. And mostly, I've looked into the vacant eyes of women who've given their souls away time and again to men in sex. I guess I care about women too much not to speak up. The *Sex and the City* message that says, "It's just sex" is just a lie.

God's Design for Sex

I need to make one thing crystal clear: God is pro-sex. Wait, let me rephrase that: God loves sex. I realize I need to make this clarification because I know many readers will assume that the point of this chapter is "Sex is bad, so just don't do it." THAT IS NOT THE MESSAGE! The real point is that sex is wonderful. God designed it and He says it is good, like everything else that He designed. But, He created it for a purpose and for our good.

Sex is like fire. Fire is incredible. Fire is life-sustaining, life-enhancing. From it we get warmth, light, sustenance, and comfort. But, fire can also be extremely dangerous. Miles of forests can be destroyed with a single, careless spark. Homes filled with family treasures—or worse, homes filled with families—are lost each day because someone played with fire in an inappropriate way. Fire isn't bad, but people who are careless with fire often reap devastating results—and not always only for themselves.

That being said, what does the Bible, God's Designer Manual, say about sex?

While *Sex and the City's* message is that sex is just a recreational activity, God's message is that sex is a profound mystery, a glorious union between a man and a woman. Sex is a blending of souls and is not to be tampered with in an unholy fashion. The Bible says:

> *There's more to sex than mere skin on skin. Sex is as much spiritual mystery as physical fact. As written in Scripture, "The two become one." . . .*
>
> *[W]e must not pursue the kind of sex that avoids commitment and intimacy, leaving us more lonely than ever—the kind of sex that can never "become one."*
>
> *There is a sense in which sexual sins are different from all others. In sexual sin we violate the sacredness of our own bodies, these bodies that were made for God-given and God-modeled love, for "becoming one" with another.*
> 1 Corinthians 6:16–18 MSG

Cameron Diaz's character, Julie, in the movie *Vanilla Sky* says something that sounds very similar to the biblical view on sex when she says the following to Tom Cruise's character, David, with whom she has had sex: "Don't you know that when you sleep with someone, your body makes a promise whether you do or not?"

Sex outside of God's design—one man and one woman for life—has devastating emotional and physical consequences. Despite what our favorite television shows and movies might teach us, there are real-life consequences that real women face, which don't easily resolve at the end of a thirty-minute program. These issues, for many women, are life changing.

> *"Don't you know that when you sleep with someone, your body makes a promise whether you do or not?"*
> —Julie,
> *Vanilla Sky*

God's design for sex is for our good. He created sex to bond a man and a woman together in the context of marriage. In the Bible, we are told that in marriage "a man leaves his father and his mother, and shall cleave unto his wife: and they shall be one flesh" (Gen. 2:24 KJV). To become one flesh implies the union of man and woman in a sexual relationship. In the original language of this verse (Hebrew), the word for *cleave* is the same word as for *glue*. God designed sex to be a bonding mechanism, or the super glue between the husband and wife, in which they become *one*. Literally, when two people have sex, their souls unite and they bond to one another in a mysterious way. This bonding works beautifully within the context of marriage. But outside of marriage, this bonding can cause emotional heart-ache and deep, lasting damage to the soul.

Emotional Consequences

The other day I went to my local grocery store to buy my weekly essentials: 2 percent milk, coffee, choc-olate graham crackers, pink lady apples, Honey Nut Cheerios, and the latest edition of *People* magazine. As I stood in line at the checkout, I couldn't help but notice the other magazine covers. It seems sex edu-cation is everywhere. *Cosmopolitan* educates its read-ers on the best way to spice up a sex life with a new trick for the New Year. *Glamour* has the "thirty things every girl should know about sex before she's thirty." *Allure* teaches women "how to look their best in the AM after an unplanned hook-up." So much informa-tion, but ironically not one single magazine headline read, "How to put your heart back together after you've given it away."

The one thing that is never taught in women's magazines is the emotional damage caused by sex out-side of God's design. Ben Young, the author of many books on dating and relationships, says, "There is no such thing as a condom for the heart." What's inter-esting is that Carrie Bradshaw came to the very same conclusion on *Sex and the City*:

*Later that night I got to thinking about safe
sex. Odd, how only when our physical life is at
risk do we follow certain guidelines to protect ourselves, but what about our emotional lives? . . .
even if you take all the precautions and emotionally try to protect yourself, when you crawl in bed
with someone, is sex ever safe?*
                    Season 3, episode 41, "Running with Scissors"

Carrie realized, as many women do, that she can try
to protect herself physically from the consequences of
sex outside of marriage, but there is just absolutely no
way to protect her heart.

A sexual revolution blew through America in the
late 1960s and 1970s. And just like the American
Revolution of 1776, with the "shot heard round the
world," this sexual revolution had its own repercus-
sions that still reverberate today. Gone were the days
of saving sex for marriage; now women believed they
were free. Birth control brought freedom from the fear
of pregnancy, and decreasing moral standards brought
freedom from guilt and shame. But years later, it is easy
to see that freedom did ring, but it was freedom from
the very things women desire most.

In a world of sex outside God's design, sure women
have the freedom to have sex with anyone at anytime,
but they are also free from the very things their hearts

desire, such as commitment, faithfulness, respect, and real love. The sexual revolution is really a prescription for sexual misery for women. Why? It's a matter of basic biology.

When a couple engages in the physical act of sex, hormones are released in both the male and female. In the woman, a powerful hormone called oxytocin is released; this hormone is what causes women to emotionally bond and glue to the man. The more oxytocin is released, the more bonding ensues. Researchers know that oxytocin is produced naturally in the brain and that it is released when a couple becomes physically intimate, most especially during sexual orgasm, producing strong bonding in both men and women. For women, it increases trust and immediately produces feelings of attachment.[1]

There is also a powerful hormone released in men during sex called vasopressin. Vasopressin is often called the "monogamy gene." This hormone is what causes a man to feel protective toward and want to provide for the woman with whom he is having sex.

But when a man and woman engage in sex outside of marriage, these hormones designed by God to create a strong, lasting marriage actually begin to work against the couple, causing mistrust, insecurity, and abandonment.[2]

Oxytocin causes a woman to cling to the man she

is physically involved with, while vasopressin causes a man to feel the necessity of commitment. If he is not obligated to her (i.e., marriage), the hormone causes him to "freak out" and pull back from the relationship. Hence the tug-of-war that is so perfectly illustrated on *Sex and the City* begins—Carrie wants more; Big wants space.

In one episode of *Sex and the City* ("Evolution"), Carrie asks herself why she can't seem to be satisfied with a "sex without strings" relationship with Mr. Big. She analyzes her desire for more and his lack of real commitment and wonders, *Is my view of a relationship extinct?* Carrie's view is not extinct. Her expectation is right, and her desire for a real commitment with the man she's having sex with is simply part of her God-given design as a woman.

In marriage the attachment created by oxytocin and vasopressin helps a couple stay connected and deal with the natural difficulties and human flaws that inevitably arise from living with another person (e.g., loving a guy who leaves the toilet seat up, who gains twenty pounds, and who forgets your birthday). But, forming such a sexual attachment in an unmarried relationship leads to several significant risks:

1. When a relationship between a man and woman ends and the sexual bond is broken, intense emotional pain occurs.

2. Repeated forming and breaking of such bonds through casual sex or multiple long-term sexual partners lessen a person's ability to bond rightly in future relationships.

3. When a woman bonds sexually to a man, she often mistakes this bond for real love and could marry the wrong person. Sex literally masks the true problems in a relationship.

4. Women often find themselves "stuck" in an unhealthy relationship because their hearts are super-glued to a guy who isn't good for them. (We've all seen a girl—or perhaps you are that girl—caught in an unhealthy relationship saying that she can't leave because she loves him. Or the couple that knows they are not right for each other and break up, then get back together, then break up again repeatedly. What keeps them returning to the scene of the crime? Often it is the pull of the sexual attachment.)[3]

A good friend of mine told me about the pain she felt after she and her long-term boyfriend broke up. "I'd had a few serious relationships end before this one. But this breakup was different. I'd had sex with this guy. All I can say is, I think my soul married him. No, we didn't walk an aisle or speak aloud any vows, but something in my heart committed to him every time we had sex. After we broke up and I saw him talking to other girls, it felt like someone took a thousand knives and slowly stabbed my heart. I've never known a pain so intense."

My friend went on to describe feelings of deep insecurity and intense self-doubt that resulted from her sexual relationship. Even though their sex was consensual, after the relationship ended, she felt used, discarded, and betrayed. Over time, she not only felt this way about herself, but also she began to see herself as usable—an object to be consumed and discarded.

When a person has sex with someone, he or she gives part of themselves away to that other person. Doing this over and over again with multiple partners chips away at a healthy self-esteem and self-respect. Another girlfriend of mine said, "When the relationship ends, it's more than just the realization that you were *one* with that person; it was like I lost myself. I was melded with that man. When he walked out the door, I went with him. It took years to find me again."

After the separation, many girls are left feeling empty, lonely, and worthless. These emotions can result in a vicious cycle. Once the insecurity takes over, girls often resort to new sexual encounters to combat the emptiness and loneliness they now feel. Many women try to convince themselves that they just don't care (Samantha Jones, for instance). Others build huge walls of defense to protect themselves against the emotional pain. These defensive walls keep them from experiencing the true love and intimacy they desire. Regardless of the response, none of this emotional destruction is God's will for women. God's design for sex is for our good, and when we follow His guidelines, we don't reap this kind of emotional turmoil.

Physical Consequences

A friend of mine suffers from a sexually transmitted disease. You'd never know it by looking at her. She's so beautiful. She's so *normal*. But every day she faces the reality that she has a virus that will never go away. One thing I love about my friend is her passion for truth. It angers her to hear the messages our media send to women about sex. You see, she knows all too well that sex outside of God's design isn't safe. She realizes there are millions of women out there just like her, women who suffer in the dark because no one told them the danger of premarital sex. Sure, she probably heard "use a condom," but the fact of the matter is most people are careless, and condoms aren't 100 percent effective—not even close.

Here are a few things our favorite TV shows and magazines don't teach us about sex:[4]

- Today, there are approximately twenty-five sexually transmitted diseases. (P.S. Ladies, there were only two known STDs in 1960.) It is estimated that one in five Americans is currently infected with one or more viral STDs. (Let's do the math: if you are out and you see ten cute guys, chances are that at least two of them have an STD. Can you tell by looking which ones have it?)

- Each day 41,000 Americans contract a sexually transmitted disease.
- *Chlamydia*, particularly dangerous to women (the number-one cause of infertility), is now the most common STD in the country. A single episode of Chlamydia PID can result in a 25 percent chance of infertility. With a second infection, the chance of infertility rises to 50 percent.
- *HPV Human Papillomavirus* (genital warts): Twenty-four million Americans may have HPV, yet more than 76 percent of women in the United States have never heard of this sexually transmitted virus that causes virtually 100 percent of all cervical cancers. (CANCER! No one ever tells us that sex outside of God's design literally destroys your body from the inside out.)
- *Genital HPV* has a particular affinity for young women. Condoms do little to protect against this common STD. Approximately one-third of unmarried sexually active people have contracted herpes by the age of thirty. Most people

who develop herpes in the genital area will continue to have outbreaks for the rest of their lives.

- *Hepatitis B* is known to be one of the most common STDs in the world. As a result of sexual intercourse, 100,000 people annually are infected with Hepatitis B.

- *HIV/AIDS* is a viral infection that selectively attacks immune cells in the human body. Experts have described it as an almost perfect "killing machine." Most people say, "It will never happen to me." But today, AIDS is the leading cause of death in Americans ages twenty-five to forty-four. Twenty-five percent of newly diagnosed HIV patients are below age twenty-two.[5] A 1995 study done by Johns Hopkins School of Medicine in Brazil showed that of 162 women who had sex with HIV-positive men, 31 developed HIV in spite of the fact that they always used condoms. Another study done by Dr. Susan Weller from the University of Texas School of Medicine showed that condoms had an average failure rate of 31 percent in preventing the transmission of HIV from an infected partner to an uninfected partner.

There is only one way to practice safe sex: "have sex with only one person and make sure that person is having sex with only you. If the two of you are together for the rest of your lives, neither one of you has to worry about any STD."

Statistics, percentages, facts—they seem cold, distant, and easy to dismiss. After all, they are only numbers. But behind every number is a face, and behind every face is a story. Here is the real-life story of a girl who knows all too well the emotional and physical consequences of sex outside of God's design.

Ashley's Story

To say I was goal oriented is an understatement. I always knew I wanted to be a cheerleader—you should have seen my back handspring. I set my mind to make the honor roll and student council officer—I accomplished both. I always hoped I would be the homecoming queen—I still have the crown. But there is one thing I never imagined I would become, and that was the girl in the waiting room of an abortion clinic.

How did I get there?

I was not a slut. Not yet anyway. Quite the contrary. I was in love and thought I was getting married. No, this is not the story of the one-time slipup. Sure, I was sexually active. But it was with my boyfriend. Every girl in my sorority slept with her boyfriend. And I was the homecoming queen, for heaven's sake. It was all so normal. Love on campus. Football sweethearts. Summer love. Young love. Great bodies. Great smiles. Shiny hair and pom-poms. And a half dozen abortion clinics within walking distance of campus.

No one told me it would be so painful. The doctor and nurses chatted and joked while they pried open my cervix. In reality, it took only a few minutes, but I felt like I was there an eternity. The machine went to work and my "problem" went away.

Everything changed.

The relationship ended. It seemed my boyfriend and I couldn't communicate anymore. We broke up a few weeks after the abortion. Something inside my soul died that day. I only thought I was empty before. Words cannot describe the black hole my soul became after the abortion. No boyfriend, no baby—I was miserable and alone.

I emerged from that experience a different woman. Gone was the cheerleader with a bright smile and high hopes. The woman who surfaced from the pool of regret and shame was hard, tough, and cold. I was so emotionally numb that it was easier just to stop feeling. So I did. I didn't feel anything.

Men became conquests, not lovers. Sex was about control, not love. I'd go out at night hoping a hook-up with a guy would give me an ego boost. Then the next morning I'd wake up with even less self-respect than I had the night before. But, it didn't seem to stop me. Now, I was easy. I didn't think very much of myself. Anyone could have sex with me and they knew it.

The drugs helped to soothe my heartache for a little while.

I started doing cocaine casually at first. Everyone in my circle was a social user. But after "the incident" I needed it more and more. I desperately needed an escape from my reality.

As it would happen, I started dating the campus drug connection. Easy access. Six months later I was pregnant again. This time I didn't tell anyone. Not the guy, not a friend. I just made the phone call to the clinic and went through the whole scenario again.

I was so out of control. It was easy this time around. This started a whole year of even more

degrading sexual activity. Guys I wouldn't
have looked at three years before I was now
going home with on a regular basis. One-night
stands, random hook-ups. Two-week flings.

My heart stopped being broken. It was too
numb to notice.

Then one night I overdosed on cocaine. I
was spiraling and spinning into a deep abyss.
God used a trip to the ER to talk some sense
into me. A nurse looked at me and said, "You
are going to die if you don't stop." You can't
hide from dying. I woke up.

I dropped out of college just a semester shy
of graduation. I went home, back to my old
bedroom filled with all the accolades of the
girl I once was and the girl I could have been.
I sat in that room surrounded by old prom cor-
sages and pageant trophies, fell on my knees,
and cried out to God for help.

Ashley came to the end of herself, and she cried
out to God for help. So, how does God respond to a
girl like Ashley? The Bible tells us how Jesus reacted to
a girl much like my friend.

How Does God Respond to a Girl Like Ashley?

Dust swirled about the crowded street as angry men dragged her from her bedroom into the broad daylight. Busted. Caught in the very act of adultery. In that culture, sex was not only assumed to be for marriage, but also adultery was punishable by death. This moment wasn't really about her though—or the man with whom she was sleeping. This moment was a trap set for Jesus. Would He uphold the law, or would He pardon the condemned?

Condemned, she was for sure. The men who dragged her into the temple courtyard seethed with contempt and scorn. They judged her actions and called for punishment.

"Stone her!" they cried. And then all eyes turned to Jesus. What would Jesus do?

The woman stood before Him, haggard. Head down, afraid to look up, and too ashamed to do so. She wasn't proud or angry . . . she was hurt. She'd been looking for love, and this is what she'd found instead. Where was the man she was sleeping with? He certainly wasn't there to defend her. Alone and afraid, she awaited her accusers.

These religious leaders really didn't care about her; it was Jesus they were interested in. She was just a pawn in their little game of religious chess. Would Jesus walk into their carefully crafted trap?

Jesus knew their motives, just as He knows every heart. Instead of facing their challenge head on, Jesus slowly and deliberately began to write on the ground. What did He write that day? Some speculate He wrote the Ten Commandments; others think He wrote the words He spoke to the crowd: "He who is without sin can cast the first stone."

Silence.

Stone silence.

Jesus did it again. Stunning the crowd and confounding the guilty, He met their challenge and opened their eyes to see the situation as He did—through eyes of mercy. A light dawned in darkened hearts. The Scripture tells us that one by one the men dropped their stones and walked away, each realizing that they had no grounds to condemn this woman to death for they, too, had sinned.

So, back to our question: How does God respond to a girl like Ashley who has fallen into sexual sin? He responds to her with the offer of grace and a new beginning. In the conclusion to this story (John 8:2–12), Jesus turned to the woman after all of her condemners had walked away and asked her, "Woman, where are they? Has no one condemned you?" She replied, "No one, Lord." And Jesus said to her, "Neither do I condemn you; go and sin no more."

Forgiveness and grace—that is the message of Jesus Christ. He reaches out to us in our pain, shame, and brokenness and offers us a fresh start. He realizes that looking for love in a hook-up is emotionally and physically devastating to us. That is why He comes to set us free from the lies that hold us captive and to give us new life.

> *Forgiveness and grace— that is the message of Jesus Christ.*

The Rest of Ashley's Story . . .

Jesus met me there.

In my high-school bedroom, just a shadow of the girl I once was, Jesus took the broken pieces of my life and He made me a new creation. The Bible says God gives us "beauty for ashes." My life was definitely in rubble and ashes—and years later, I can tell you He has made it something beautiful.

Jesus desires to give every woman who has been looking for love in sex what He gave to my friend Ashley and to the woman caught in adultery—He wants to give you a fresh start. Only Jesus can do this; He is the God of new beginnings. He is the only One who is able to take the broken pieces of our lives and make us whole. Jesus wants the *rest of your story* to be something beautiful. I know this one from experience.

The Secret to a Fresh Start

I know many women who've realized that sex outside God's design just doesn't work. They aren't clueless; they can see the consequences for what they are, yet they just don't know how to change. So how do they change? How does this "fresh start" that Christ offers work? If they've received His forgiveness and grace, there is only one requirement, and that is to see themselves as Christ sees them. Jesus Christ sees them as a treasure worth dying for.

They are not trash; they are a treasure. A treasure is something we prize and carefully protect. But trash is something we throw away when we are finished using it. Dispensable. The sad thing is, many women in our culture have grown so accustomed to being treated like trash that it feels normal.

It's easy to see why, in our culture, women face strong opposing messages when it comes to sex. On one hand, as we've discussed, we get the message that "sex is just sex." Sex is no big deal. Hopefully by now we understand that sex is a *really* big deal. God designed it to be a glorious union of souls. When we buy the lie that says, "It's just sex," and tell ourselves, *I shouldn't care that he won't commit or has moved on to another girl,* we settle for so much less than God's best. We should care!!! We are worth much more than that kind of treatment. Our Designer created us for something much more glori- ous. God wants us with men who are committed to us for life and who see us as Christ sees us.

> What message are we sending if we allow ourselves to be treated as a something *instead of a* someone?

On the other hand, we are bombarded with another dangerous message: a woman's worth is found in being desired sexually by a man. Many women build their self-esteem on being an object of sexual desire. They think it is a compliment if a man wants to use them for sex. It's gotten to the point that some actu- ally believe it is flattering to be objectified. Gone are the days when women respected themselves enough to get angry when treated like an object. Today we not only expect it, but many actually like it. (Has anyone out there seen a "Girls Gone Wild" TV commercial? Case closed.) But let's think about this: What message are we sending if we allow ourselves to be treated as a *something* instead of a *someone?* We are saying, "It's OK to use me. I'm just an object."

You are someone. Think about that word *object.* An object is something that is used. Is that really what you want? Do you want to be something that is simply used for someone else's pleasure? Or, do you want more? I think most women want much more . . . and guess what? God wants more for us too.

God says to women, "You are a priceless treasure. You are worth fighting for. You are worth waiting for." Do you hear these words? Better yet, do you believe these words? In order for you to have a fresh start, you must believe one fundamental truth about yourself: you must believe that you are, in fact, a treasure. You are worth more than a casual hook-up. You are worth more than just satisfying someone's physical pleasure. You are worth more than being used and forgotten.

God's view of sex is so grand that He has one basic command and that is this: any man who is worthy of having sex with you should be willing to die for you. *Die for me?* I know that sounds extreme, but it really isn't. Sure, I realize we live in a world where people have sex without even knowing each other's last names, but that is a degraded abuse. Sex was created for the lifelong commitment of marriage. According to the Bible, in marriage the husband is to love his wife as Jesus Christ loves the church—the church is not a building; it is the group of people who have faith in Jesus Christ (Eph. 5:25).

Translation, girls: Jesus died for the church. Literally, Christ died for us. Instead of our deaths for our sins, Christ died for us. Scripture says, "For God loved the world in this way: He gave His One and Only Son, so that everyone who believes in Him will not perish but have eternal life" (John 3:16). Jesus Christ gave His life up for you and me. And this sacrificial love is the model God gives for men in a marriage. God is essentially saying to us, "The man who is worthy of having sex with you is the man who is willing to die for you." Sacrificial, selfless, put-your-needs-first kind of love—that is God's best for you. That is a far cry from being an object.

So ladies, my question is this: why would we ever settle for anything less than God's best? I realize millions of women are out at bars and clubs across the world wondering which guy they will hook up with. The hunger for love leads many women to search for intimacy in a hook-up and settle for a few hours of physical connection. Most women don't want the proverbial one-night stand, but the sad fact is that *one night* is about all these women will get. Like a bumper sticker I read one time, they are "Looking for love but will settle for sex."

God wants you to be with a man who will not only be there in the morning, but one who will also be there *every* morning. God wants you to be with someone who will love you and not use you. The love you are looking for will never be found in the sex-without-strings lifestyle that is portrayed by Samantha on *Sex and the City*. You give up so much when you give in. You give away your own worth. You give away your mystery. You give away your soul. God wants so much more for you. Why? Because, my friend, *you* are His treasure.

Is God's Way Really Worth Waiting For?

I'll be really honest with you; I almost ended the chapter with the previous paragraph. I could have and been happy with the content, but something inside me said, "Wait . . . there's still a big question looming." Then I thought about it. If I were reading this book, what would I still need to hear? What question would I want to ask? Quick recap: So far we've talked about the negative consequences of going against God's design. And we've also discussed the importance of a woman knowing her true value as a treasure in order to have a fresh start. But the one thing I've failed to mention is this: why God's way is worth waiting for.

In case you haven't picked up on this little fact yet, I'm still single. So my perspective on sex inside of marriage (God's design) is, how shall I say this, somewhat limited. I can tell you the negative consequences of going against His design, but to be flat-out honest, I can't tell you the beauty of God's design from firsthand experience. Until God blesses me with marriage, I've asked one of my best friends to share her story.

I close this chapter about looking for love in a hook-up with her story of waiting, trusting, and believing that God's design for sex is good. This is a testimony of a woman who knows firsthand that God's way is really worth waiting for.

Susannah—A Lady Who Waited

Growing up, if I heard it once, I heard it a thousand times: "What looks like rejection is God's protection." It was my mom's answer to every formal I wasn't asked to (including my senior prom), every dance I didn't dance, every cute guy who looked once and never looked back again. But looking back, after five years of marriage to the most incredible man I know, Mom was right.

She was right when I didn't want her to be right. She was right when it hurt to be right. She was right because every time a guy said "no" to me because I wasn't the sex object he wanted, by following God's design for sex, He was saving me for my future husband and, most significantly, for Himself.

When I met my husband, I was twenty-three years old; he was twenty-nine. Both of us were virgins, and when I say virgins, I mean virgins. "First base" (a.k.a. kissing) was as far as

either of us had ever been, and throughout our
two years of dating, that's as far as we ever went.
Why? Was it because my husband was less of
a man than other men? No. Was it because he
was unattractive? No; far from it. He is one of
the most handsome men I know. It was because
we both took God at His word, and when He
said, "Wait. Abstain. Forgo pleasure now for
pleasure later," we believed Him.

And God was right. If you've never seen
the most recent film version of Jane Austen's
novel *Pride and Prejudice*, go rent it. It's worth
every penny. During one of the last scenes in
the movie, the heroine, Elizabeth Bennett,
is miserable in her waiting. She has spent a
sleepless night waiting to see if Mr. Darcy,
the man she loves, still loves her. She greets
the dawn outside in the cold morning mists,
and as the mists part, she looks up to see Mr.
Darcy striding through the fields coming to
claim her as his bride.

That, my friends, is what sex feels like
on your wedding night and throughout
marriage when you have waited. Pure
Passion. Unimaginable Beauty. Sacred
Ground. There are no regrets when the only
sexual partner either of you has ever had is

each other. There are no imaginations of the other women he has been with or the other men who have shared your bed. There is no fear of "the morning after." When I go to bed, my husband is there. When I wake up in the morning, he is there. There is no shame. No comparison of our bodies to others. No regret. No remorse. We are free—free to enjoy one another without the chains of past wounds, past hurts, past sexual emotional bondage.

What I am not saying is that our marriage is perfect or that waiting to have sex was easy. Marriage, at times, is hard, very hard. Waiting to have sex was hard. Being picked over, passed over, looked over for other girls who were more willing was hard. Controlling our passions in the heat of the moment and stopping to say, "No" when everything in our bodies was screaming, "Yes!" was hard, very hard. But harder still would have been waking up the next morning realizing that I had disobeyed God, betrayed my true Lover, and not waited.

And the significance of our wait only grows more beautiful with time, for the further along we are into marriage, the more thankful I am that we waited. When I don't

have to worry about where Jason is or what
he is doing, because I know he is able to
wait, I am thankful. When I don't have to
struggle with where his eyes look when a
pretty woman passes or where my eyes turn
when a good-looking man walks by because
we have learned the discipline of waiting only
for each other, I am thankful. God's design
for sex within marriage, for one man to be
united with one woman, works. I have seen
it, firsthand, to be for our protection. I know
I can trust my husband because I know he is
trustworthy. Because he treated me as a treasure while we dated, I trust that he will be
faithful throughout our marriage. Our culture
might call it old-fashioned, outdated, archaic,
unliberated, or even ridiculous, but let me tell
you from one woman to another, God's way is
beautiful . . . and yes, I feel treasured.

~ ~ ~

I hope Susannah's story is an encouragement to you.
If you've decided to wait until marriage for sex, stay the
course. God's design is for your good and greatest joy.
But remember, never stop expecting men to treat you
like a treasure . . . you are worth waiting for.

If you are reading this and you haven't waited, don't

despair—it's never too late. There is no such thing as "too late" with Jesus. Jesus is the God of new beginnings. God's grace cleanses and forgives all sin. The Bible says, "There is now no condemnation for those who are in Christ Jesus" (Rom. 8:1 NIV). When you sincerely come to Christ desiring a fresh start, He doesn't condemn (judge, ridicule, or scorn) you. Jesus came to heal you. Jesus wants to heal the emotional wounds and the physical destruction you endured from sex outside of God's design. And get this, God also desires to shower you with His love so that you will know that *you*, yes you, are His treasure.

> *Never stop expecting men to treat you like a treasure . . . you are worth waiting for.*

One of my favorite things about Jesus is that He was a carpenter by trade while on earth. Why do I love this truth? Because a carpenter is someone who rebuilds and restores—he is in the construction business. When we give our lives to Jesus, He takes pleasure in the reconstruction of a life. He absolutely loves to take a life and make something new—transforming the broken into the beautiful. This one, my friends, I do know from experience.

At the end of this book you will find keys to the transformation that Jesus longs to do in your life. This isn't a "to-do list" but helpful hints from one girl, who once was looking for love, to another. Jesus has transformed my life, and it is my greatest joy to share with you how He can make your life something beautiful too.

chapter Six

Looking
for Love
at Happy Hour

I have low self-esteem,
but I express it the healthy way . . .
by eating a box of Double Stuf Oreos.
MIRANDA HOBBS OF *SEX AND THE CITY*

What does not satisfy when we find it,
was not the thing we were desiring.
C. S. LEWIS, *THE PILGRIM'S REGRESS*

The clock rolls to 5:00 p.m., and office buildings everywhere empty as men and women hurry to their local watering hole to let off some steam. For some it's a time to celebrate, and for others, a time to forget the cares of the day. It's happy hour, a time to throw back a few rounds of beer—or if you are Carrie Bradshaw, a few cosmopolitans—hoping to find a little liquid pick-me-up at the end of a long day. But happy hour isn't always about alcohol, is it?

Happy hour could be a buy-one-get-one-free sale at your favorite shoe store. Or it could be marathon hours in front of the television or the Internet. Still, for some, it is an all-you-can-eat buffet or hours exercising at the gym or sleeping the entire day away. It's all the same really.

Happy hour is about escaping.

Happy hour is about indulging.

Happy hour is about feeling . . . well, *happy?*

The Fix

I recently recognized my own brand of happy hour during an unusually stressful and emotionally draining week. I found myself circling a local megamall parking garage looking for a space. It was instinctive. Without thinking really, I'd hopped in my car from the office and hurried over to the great beacon of capitalism—the shopping mall. As I drove up the ramps of the parking garage and searched row by row for an empty space (praying, I might add, for a parking favor), I asked myself a question: *Why am I here?*

It had been one of those weeks. You know the kind I'm talking about, when the usual places you go looking for love are closed for business. A relationship was in turmoil (not feelin' the love there), and my career wasn't giving me the emotional props I wanted. The combo was causing sleep deprivation, and then my appearance wasn't exactly turning heads either. All the usual sources of props, praise, and admiration weren't showin' me the love. Where is a girl to run in moments like that?

Did I need anything? One look at my closet and a second glance at my checkbook would tell me the answer . . . no. What was I hoping to find in the mall that day? Would buying something new really banish my blues?

I hate it when I check my motives. It usually means I'm doing something for the wrong reason. But I'm glad I asked myself the question. You see, I was emotionally spent. A conversation with a friend left me feeling sad and hurt, and to make matters worse, I'd messed up something at work. As a result I was feeling like a failure. Sitting there in my car, I had an epiphany: I'm running to the mall to fill an ache in my heart—the ache that desires to be approved, to be noticed, to not feel rejected—the ache that longs for love. But I took my longing to the wrong place. I thought that the thrill of the purchase would make my cares disappear.

If you've watched even one episode of *Sex and the City*, you know where Carrie Bradshaw turns when she needs a little "happy hour." She grabs the credit card and visits her friends: Dolce & Gabana, Manolo Blahnik, Jimmy Choo, Calvin (Klein, that is), and of course, Chanel. Whether she's at Bergdorf's or a shop in SoHo, Carrie freely admits that shopping, especially shoe shopping, is her number-one fix when life feels broken. This should come as no surprise from a girl who calls *Vogue* her Bible. Like Carrie, most of us turn to our own version of happy hour when we are frustrated or just plain disappointed with life.

But does Carrie have the right fix? Better yet, did I?

Back to the parking garage, I'm glad I recognized the *real* issue. I've done enough emotional spending in the past to know that yet another new pair of jeans is not the answer. Escaping from reality in the aisles of designer jeans and the must-have new lip colors really doesn't fix anything. In reality, shopping therapy actually makes things worse. Eventually the credit card bill arrives, and my outfit's magical ability to make me feel good about myself is gone with the first wash.

Shopping does offer a momentary thrill, but the thrill is gone way too soon. Just like waking up with a crushing hangover after a night of too much drinking, any version of happy hour can leave you feeling wasted and dehydrated. Or broken and broke. Carrie said it best, in both diagnosing and lamenting her penchant for happy hours:

> *Eventually the credit card bill arrives, and my outfit's magical ability to make me feel good about myself is gone with the first wash.*

*I've spent $40,000 on shoes and I have no
place to live? I will literally be the old woman who
lived in her shoes!*

Season 4, episode 64, "Ring and Ding Ding"

What is it that you, Carrie, and I are really trying
to fix?

As a woman who has a relationship with Jesus
Christ, I know that my soul isn't going to be filled with
a new outfit or a great pair of slingbacks. Those things
are only temporary remedies, and the real issue will
surface again if I don't run to *real comfort*: my relationship with Jesus. (More on how we do this later.)

Comfort Zones

It seems I'm not the only one who's had an epiphany. Recently I heard Sarah "Fergie" Ferguson discussing why she became the Weight Watchers spokes-
person. She admitted that years of "comfort eating" had
become a way of life, a lifestyle that required intense
training and mental discipline to overcome. Comfort
eating became her comfort zone. That phrase stuck
in my brain. It's the same thing. Spending, eating,
drinking . . . all of these things come down to a feeble
attempt to feel good and pacify some emptiness.

Who hasn't used food, or should I say abused food,
as a means of filling the soul? A close friend described
to me her own emotional relationship with food by

saying, "I've dieted for years. Every fad diet or pill that hits the market . . . I've tried it (sometimes more than once). But I've discovered the real issue is my relationship with food, not the food I eat. For years, I turned to food to feel *better*. My 'happy hour' was boxes of cookies and other snacks. Like medicine for a headache, I used food for a heartache. Sure, I was hungry, but it wasn't a hunger for food. I was grasping at everything food represented: warm memories, celebrations, love, family, home, safety, and security. I found when my heart was hurting or life was spinning out of control, the stronger the pull was to the pantry. Or when numbness had settled over my entire life, even the briefest sensuality of flavor, a good taste on my tongue, jolted my flatlining heart for a life-saving moment. But the fix never proved sustainable, and despondency always returned."

Just like the character Miranda Hobbs, who indulged in chocolate cake and Oreos as her comfort zone, my friend's way of feeding her insecurity was with food.

That word *comfort* seems to be popping up everywhere these days. In one of the extremely intellectual publications of our day, *In-Touch Weekly Magazine*, there is an article about a famous Hollywood actress. The article analyzes her relationship woes and labels her recent spending binges as comfort shopping. The actress is reported to have spent over $15,000 in one outing to Barney's in Beverly Hills. The point isn't the price tag (I'm sure she could afford this much and more); the point is the purpose. Even the writer of the article questions whether she is shopping to fill some emptiness inside.

What I've noticed about looking for love at happy hour is this: most of the people just aren't happy. I know this from experience. Sure, there are good times to be had. All the things we are talking about in this chapter can be good things used in a bad way. Let's take food, for instance. Food is great. God gave us food to nourish our bodies and for enjoyment, but if I am turning to food as my comfort zone, then I will have an unhealthy relationship with food. The same can be said of anything that God created. Nothing or no one but God alone is able to fill His place in our lives.

The Eyes

I have a box of old photos from my happy-hour days. Photos of the "old me" double-fisting and surrounded by others who were using substances to numb the ache. A time when hitting the bars was a given and when my life revolved around getting a good buzz. When I look at pictures of the girl I once was, I see past the fact that I look older today; I see a different set of eyes staring back at me. The girl in those pictures has a big smile, but if you look closely, you'll see it isn't real. Sure, she's

> I thought if I could convince everyone else I was having a good time, then maybe, just maybe, I'd believe it myself. But you couldn't escape my eyes; they told a different story.

at a party, and she probably wasn't feeling too much when the photo was snapped, but those eyes—they tell the true story.

If you had seen me then, you would've seen a girl who was desperately trying to be the life of the party. Always trying to be fun, cute, and oh-so-entertaining. I thought if I could convince everyone else I was having a good time, then maybe, just maybe, I'd believe it myself. But you couldn't escape my eyes; they told a different story.

And my eyes were . . .

Hollow.

Vacant.

Empty.

Blank.

Lifeless.

It seems the more I attempted to squeeze life out of a bottle, the more I lost myself. Even Laura Mercier (or for you country girls like me, Mary Kay) can't put a sparkle of real joy *in* the eyes.

I see the same vacant expression staring back at me in photos of one of the most famous women in America. Her picture is flashed across magazine covers and her life is chronicled each day on news reports. She is a walking example of happy hour gone bad. Her recent escapades from divorce court to party girl have caused quite a stir. It seems each day a new story surfaces of her wild behavior. While I hate the tabloid sensationalism that surrounds this girl, I will say she is giving women everywhere a good look at the downward spiral of a life fed by drugs and alcohol. The sad thing to me is that it is such a waste. How sad to watch a beautiful and talented young woman go to such incredible and humiliating lengths in her search for love.

Here's the main problem with looking for love at happy hour—there's never enough. There's never enough food to fill the soul. Have you ever stood in front of the refrigerator and said, "I'm not hungry, but I really want to eat"? That is the soul hunger. Have you ever spent too much money shopping and later realized that you were spending to feel better? And then there are the substances. *Clearly*, narcotics and other drugs are harmful and dangerous in their own right, but the motive behind using them is this: to numb and escape the pain and emptiness of life. But here's the catch: the more someone uses, the more they have to use because the core problem is still there—an empty soul.

Running on Empty

To say I'm a little scatterbrained is an understatement. I lose my keys at least once a week. More than likely the bottom of my purse (if I can find it) is a jumble of old bills, sticky notes, Sweet-n-Low packages, broken lipstick, and a few thank-you notes that I thought I'd already mailed. That's me. I've tried to reform my ways. I've tried organizers, memory systems, and little reminders on my mirror, but, in the end, I am who I am—creative and keyless. Self-acceptance is a beautiful thing, except when you run out of gas.

You would think I would have seen the bright orange light flashing in front of me. If memory serves, I think I did notice something a few days back, but I was too busy to do anything about it. You see, it was wedding season. And when I say "wedding season," I mean SEASON! I single-handedly (pun intended) attended eleven weddings in twelve weeks. Pile on top of the wedding ceremonies the ever-so-important bridesmaid luncheons, lingerie parties, kitchen showers, rehearsal dinners, and couples showers. And not to mention the fact that a girl still has to hold down a full-time job in order to pay for all the china, blenders, and bridesmaid dresses. Who has time to remember a silly thing like filling up a gas tank?

Obviously I didn't because at 7:23 a.m. when I should have already rolled out of my local Starbucks, I was instead slowly rolling through an intersection as my car sputtered to a dead stall. I was out of gas. Hear me—not just low running low—flat out empty. As a shriek left my lips, I looked around to find a safe place to coast my now dead car. Right in front of me awaited my car's destination: the local funeral home.

I ran out of gas at a funeral home! The lesson didn't hit me until later that afternoon when, equipped with five dollars worth of unleaded in a stylin' new purse-sized gas can, a friend drove me back to get my car. As we pulled into the parking lot, the symbolism hit me square between the eyes. This whole fiasco was a great illustration of my life before Jesus Christ.

I was going fast, running on empty, and heading straight for a place of death. My life before Jesus consisted of the fuel of the world: momentary pleasure and the quick *I ran out of gas at a funeral home!* fix of a good buzz to get me through—fueling my life with whatever I thought would make me happy. But the more I ran on this fuel, the more empty my life felt, and, like my car, there was one sure destination awaiting me.

Is there anyone reading this right now who, for one moment, paused when you read "funeral home" and had the briefest shadow flicker across your soul? Was there a hint of recognition or a creepy sensation that just maybe you are in danger of running out of gas in that dark and undesirable place? A place where mere memories are the only vestiges left of a once-joyful life and where tears and disappointment are the currency now tendered, but the time has passed and no amount of remorse can refill the tank. The Bible says, "There is a way that seems right to a man, but in the end it leads to death" (Prov. 14:12 NIV).

How's your soul's fuel light? Perhaps the lifestyle I was living wouldn't have ended in physical death, but it sure was a death to so many other things: my joy, my potential, my self-worth, and ultimately death to the woman God created me to be. I was heading down a path of destruction.

How's your soul's fuel light? Do you recognize the warning signs of emptiness, or are you too busy, too distracted, and too dazed to notice? Girls, I'm gonna shoot straight with you. None of the fuel stations of the world ever fill the tank. The reason is our tanks need more filling than food and more satisfying than any substance . . . we are crying out for God. And when we turn to these empty substitutes to fill the God-spot, we can end up imprisoned to them. How does happy hour become a prison? Because the reality is that it always takes more each time to feel happy.

Happy hour can easily turn into an addiction: shopping addicts, food addicts, TV addicts, drug addicts, exercise addicts, sex addicts, approval addicts, sleep addicts, people addicts, and any other thing we use to pacify our souls' addictions. Our little happy hours (a.k.a. your comfort zones) can actually imprison us. Shopping to fill the void can imprison us to financial debt. Eating or starving to fill the void can imprison us to weight and health issues. Using substances (drugs or alcohol) to fill the void can literally send us to prison. And any other means we use and abuse to make us feel whole, complete, and secure takes a powerful grip on our lives. We keep returning to our comfort zones until the zone itself becomes an uncomfortable cell. Once we become dependent, we use it more and more and more. I am absolutely EXHAUSTED being *this happy* . . . how 'bout you?

Intervention

One time I heard a girl articulate so clearly why her version of happy hour turned into an addiction, one that she knew full well was destroying her life. She said, "Something was inherently wrong with me that needed to be filled, made whole, or patched." Did you hear what she said? This girl identified the real problem; her addiction was simply a way to "patch" the ache. Wasn't she right? Like a nicotine patch for a smoker, we use so many substitutes to pacify the real longing of our soul.

I have great news. There is hope. Hope is what most of us need, isn't it? Because God loves us so much, He planned an intervention—the *original* intervention.

He hates to see the destruction in our lives, so Jesus came to free us from all the places we go looking for love apart from Him. Jesus came to give us real life, real joy, real hope, and real satisfaction. In explaining our need for an intervention, Jesus said, "The thief comes only to steal and kill and destroy; I have come that they may have life, and have it to the full" (John 10:10 NIV). Who is the thief? The thief is Satan. Since the beginning, Satan has been trying to rob humanity of its joy by separating us from our true source of life. But God's plan for relationship with us was not thwarted by Satan's deceit.

> *Our comfort zones are really just distractions of Satan to keep us from turning to God.*

When Jesus says He came that we may have "life," what He describes is much more than just mere existence. He offers vitality, richness, and fullness. Abundance. This type of life is a far cry from the type that is dependent on food, fashion, or substances to sustain its happiness. Satan, who is the thief of real life and destroyer of true joy, tempts us with all kinds of lures that promise to bring us happiness and pleasure but fail to meet our real need. A person can exist, turning to things for happiness, and never really feel alive. Our comfort zones are really just distractions of Satan to keep us from turning to God.

Second question: what does Jesus mean by *abundant?* The word picture here is a life "over and above the norm, overflowing, and filled up." This word *abundant* reminds me of a memory from my childhood. When I was a little girl, I attended my cousin's wedding. It was a fairy-tale wedding—a limo ride, the handsome groom in a black tux waiting at the end of the aisle, the smell of roses wafting through the house, and music filling the air. Spellbound, I felt as if Cinderella herself had invited me to the ball. But one of my clearest memories of this wedding was of the massive fountain that stood right in the middle of the ballroom. I'd never seen anything like it. Transfixed in my pink ruffles and white patent leather mary janes, I watched as the fountain bubbled up from within and spilled over the top—a constant motion of flowing, bubbling liquid. Far too young to understand the mechanics, I thought the fountain had a never-ending supply. Obviously it didn't, but the life Jesus offers us does.

The life Jesus describes is satisfying and overflowing with surpassing and lasting joy. And how do we get this life? Jesus tells us we get this life by believing in Him: "If anyone is thirsty, let him come to me and drink. Whoever believes in me, as the Scripture has said, streams of living water will flow from within him" (John 7:37–38 NIV). Jesus says that those who believe (place a confident trust) in Him will have a fountain of living water flow within their souls. Since water is a symbol for life, the picture is clear. Unlike happy hour with its momentary buzz, Jesus offers us a life that is filled with something much more satisfying, and lasting: Himself. I'll never forget driving in my car one afternoon after giving my life to Jesus and the thought hitting me, *I finally feel alive*. That moment is crystalized in my memory because the surge of life was a shocking contrast to the vacant existence that was mine before Christ. Remember, we are created by God and for relationship with Him. Apart from Him, we will never find the real satisfaction, joy, or life we are looking for.

Craving Connection

All of this boils down to one thing: we crave connection with our Creator. The reason we won't find true happiness at happy hour is because it just isn't there. Author C. S. Lewis, a convert from atheism to Christianity, said it best when he described man's dependency on God for life and joy as follows:

> God designed the human machine to run on Himself. He Himself is the fuel our spirits were designed to burn, or the food our spirits were designed to feed on. There is no other. That is why it is just no good asking God to make us happy in our own way without bothering about

religion. God cannot give us a happiness and
peace apart from Himself, because it is not there.
There is no such thing.

God is the fuel our spirits were designed to burn. In this quote, Lewis's words describe the final truth that Jesus gave His followers the night before He was crucified.

~ ~ ~

Torches and twilight marked the path as the bewildered disciples followed Jesus toward their destination. They trudged along the winding path with heavy hearts, not from the evening's meal but from the conversation that ensued during it. Throughout the evening Jesus prepared His followers for the events that would soon take place. He warned them of His impending suffering and death. Skeptical of the message, yet believing the messenger, the group grappled with the news shared with them this eve.

Leaving the meal the group walked along in silence until they happened upon a vineyard. Jesus knew this was His final moment with His followers before His death, and He took this time to share with them a fundamental truth.

In my opinion, a person's last words are pretty important. Final thoughts, farewells, and instructions are often given in these moments. History is full of both funny and moving last words. If the final words are from Jesus Christ, who is God Himself, then I think we should pay special attention. The following Scripture is the last lesson Jesus taught His followers before He died on the cross. The setting for this talk is a vineyard, a place where grapevines dot the lush hillside.

Keep in mind that Jesus journeyed with this group for three years. During that time He taught them many things about life: forgive those who hurt you because you, too, have been forgiven. Love others because love is the number-one characteristic of a person who knows Him. Live humbly because pride is the root of all sin. And Jesus also taught not to judge by externals but rather look at the heart of a person. This group had heard Jesus instruct them on many things, and His words of life had transformed the hearers. But as the group traveled through the vineyard, Jesus took this final moment to teach this one last and extremely important truth: for a person to have a life overflowing with true joy, that person must remain connected to the one true source of life, Jesus Christ:

> *I am the true vine, and My Father is the vine-*
> *yard keeper. Remain in Me, and I in you. Just as*
> *a branch is unable to produce fruit by itself unless*

it remains on the vine, so neither can you unless you remain in Me.

I am the vine; you are the branches. The one who remains in Me and I in him produces much fruit, because you can do nothing without Me. My Father is glorified by this: that you produce much fruit and prove to be My disciples.

As the Father has loved me, I have also loved you. Remain in My love. If you keep My commands you will remain in My love, just as I have kept My Father's commands and remain in His love.

I have spoken these things to you so that My joy may be in you and your joy may be complete.

John 15:1, 4–5, 8–11

When Jesus compares Himself to a "vine" and calls His followers "branches," the imagery is clear. Just as a branch is dependent on the vine for life, so are we dependent on Jesus for real life. The grapevine sends nourishment and food to the branches, which in turn produce abundant grapes. When we are connected to Christ, His life flows in us and through us, and the outcome is the fruit of *joy*. If we want to have the overflowing, joy-filled life that Christ offers us, we must stay connected to Him.

What does it mean to "remain" connected to Jesus? To be connected to Jesus means that He is my source of life—dependency. Like a branch that is dependent on the vine for life, the woman who is connected to Jesus receives life from Him. Her identity, her worth, her strength, her hope—all of these come from the One who is the real source of life. Instead of looking to people to define us or depending on substances for comfort, we turn to Christ and allow His love to fill our lives.

That's why He came in the first place, remember? To reconnect us with God.

When humankind was separated from God in the garden because of sin, our problem of looking for love began. Jesus came to reconnect us—to restore the joy, hope, love, life, and security that we find only in Him. We grasp at the things that represent comfort and make us feel secure because those are the very things we lost in the garden. We lost the real sense of security that tells us all is right and good in our world. That security comes from only one place.

How's It Working for You?

For the past few years I've worked with high-school students. They are hip on the new and new. They keep me updated on all the latest trends in everything from technology to fashion. Because I am a few years older (OK . . . at least a decade), what I bring to the table is "real life" experience. I've tried over the years to share with them many of the life lessons I've gathered from "looking for love in all the wrong places." Sometimes they listen, but other times I get that look—the one that says, "That would never happen to me."

It seems in high school you think you are the exception to the rule. Consequences? Those happen to other people. And when you are a teenager, there's this uncanny ability to walk around like you are bulletproof. I often laugh at their absolute confidence and sheer lack of fear.

Bulletproof thinking changes once you leave high school.

Each year I say good-bye to a graduating class and watch from afar as they enter the wilderness we call college. For most of these students it is a time of freedom and new experiences. I love it when they come home for break and share about all the amazing new people and life insights they've garnered in their time away. But every now and then, I have a talk that is difficult.

One of my favorite girls came to visit me one afternoon after a few years of being out of touch. She looked older than she should. Her face carried marks of the road she'd traveled, and her walk wasn't as confident as it was before. And in her eyes I read a familiar story.

You know the one: good girl gone wild. She was your typical overachiever—great-at-everything kind of girl. Over the years, I watched her happy hour escalate from one comfort zone to the next. In high school she was an approval addict and lived for the applause of the crowd and the approval of her peers. This fix worked for a season because she could always perform or stand out in order to get attention. But once she hit college, and she was no longer a name but now just a number, she had to find something new to make her feel good.

Binge drinking and partying were fun at first. When she drank, she felt free—free from her fears of rejection and failure—and able for a moment to overcome her social insecurities. She used alcohol to boost her confidence. But as it usually does, drinking led to other substances, and now she was using and abusing other drugs in her effort to find happiness.

As I sat and listened to her all-too-familiar tale, I waited to ask my question: "How's it working for you?" She sat a few seconds and stared blankly back at me, so I asked again, "How's it working for you? Are you happy? Does all of the stuff you are experimenting with bring you the joy and peace you are looking for?"

Her answer was, "No . . . actually I'm miserable." She understood the reason for my question. If this lifestyle isn't making you happy, why do you keep going back for more? We sat for a while and talked about why she would never find happiness in a person's approval or a bottle of anything. Our conversation turned to her soul's hunger for God and how she was looking in all the wrong places.

Hesitancy was written all over her face. She knew she needed to turn to Jesus, but she was afraid to do so. Fear of letting go of her comfort zones and fear of being different from the other girls at college kept her from turning to God. So, she walked out my door promising to think about our talk. I did not know if I would hear from her again.

Honestly, I didn't know if our chat—or this book— would actually help anything change. My prayerful desire is to make girls *aware* of what that nagging pain and emptiness actually are. But I realize each woman must come to her own conclusion about initiating the changes she needs in her life. Trust me, I fully recognize that a woman can realize she is miserable in her present condition yet not be ready to take a step of faith. I've been in that spot. When "happy hour" is all you know, it is difficult to imagine real life can be found elsewhere. Each woman must decide for herself if she is at a place where she wants change. For, tomorrow will dawn and with it will come new opportunities, new hopes, as well as old habits, fresh temptations, and the draw of the familiar. Could she—can you—actually take a new day and embrace the hope for a new brand of comfort?

Months later an e-mail arrived in my inbox. Her name jolted my attention so I quickly clicked it open.

It seems in the weeks following our talk she began to see her life and the consequences of her choices more clearly. Yes, she faced consequences: shame from her sexual promiscuity, a declining GPA and physical health because of her "extracurricular activities," and emotional emptiness that plagued her continuously. She realized that she was searching and lost without God. She told me of coming to a place of brokenness and finally realizing it "wasn't working for her."

Here's the thing: for years this girl knew information about Jesus—kind of like how we know information about a celebrity, but we don't actually *know* that person. For instance, my friends and I talk about Brad Pitt and Angelina Jolie as if they are in our social circle. However, "Brangelina" has yet to call and ask our opinion about new tattoos, new adoptions, or new film roles. The same is true of God (not the calling part, of course). A person can know stuff about Him without really believing in Him. This girl had heard stories about Jesus, but she never came to the place of true belief, where her life was connected to His life— a place of confident trust and dependency.

After returning to college, she realized the happiest place for her would be connected to her Creator. It was common sense really. She recognized she was a "branch" disconnected and withering because she wasn't connected to and receiving life from The

Vine, Jesus Christ. Awareness of the problem is only half the battle.

I'm not going to sugarcoat this one for you; her decision to change wasn't easy. Giving up our happy hour spots is never a piece of cake. But she realized as did I years before that looking for love at happy hour was wrecking her life. So, she made a decision to stop relying on alcohol for confidence, random hook-ups for intimacy, and people's opinions for props and instead chose to take Jesus at His word and give dependency upon Him a try.

Giving up our happy hour spots is never a piece of cake.

Reconnected, she finally knows freedom from the performance treadmill and substance dependency, and she is experiencing true happiness in the overflowing life of Jesus Christ. How? She's learned the secret of daily dependence. She had to. The lure to the old lifestyle can be strong even when you recognize it for what it is . . . empty. When life hits a rough patch and she needs an emotional fix, she makes the conscious decision to turn to Jesus instead of her old comfort zones. She's learned to stay close to Christ in relationship and turn to Him whenever her heart is looking for love, and guess what . . . it's working for her!

~ ~ ~

Let me close this chapter by saying something I think is extremely important for someone who fears giving up her comfort zones: following Jesus is incredible! I have more fun today as a believer in Jesus Christ than I ever did in any of my happy hour days. I say this because I know the image most people have of Christians isn't always, well . . . fun. That's not me, nor is it any of my friends. I'd say my life today is happy, but that word doesn't really scratch the surface. I'm not saying everything is perfect. Sure, I have heartbreaks, breakouts, letdowns—and even as I write these words a raging case of the cramps—just like the next girl. But now, there's something different. There is a deep current of life that runs through my soul that sustains me in the winds and storms so that even when life isn't necessarily happy, I still have joy.

Now, not only am I alert and sober enough to enjoy every minute of life, but the experiences themselves are real and satisfying. I laugh (actually, sometimes I snort). I dance (with or without music, it doesn't really matter to me. As they say in the movie *Girls Just Wanna Have Fun*, "I just love to dance"). I play, albeit I still don't like to lose, and, yes, I am happy. I feel ALIVE, not because something has given me a jolt but because *Someone* has given me life. Girls, I'm connected to my Creator, and just let me say, it is so very good.

chapter seven

He *Is*
Just That into You!

I'm not gonna sugarcoat it for you;
he's just not that into you.
JACK BERGER OF *SEX AND THE CITY*
Season 6, episode 78, "Pick a Little, Talk a Little"

t all began with the six simple words: *he's just not that into you*. Carrie Bradshaw and her current flame, Jack Berger, joined the girls for dinner to do what girlfriends do best: analyze their love lives. Carrie brought Jack there to meet her friends, who were all in their typical form. Conscious of the male presence at the table, Miranda asked Berger if he could handle all the "girl talk." Encouraged to continue, Miranda unfolds the details of a past date as Jack grows quiet. Charlotte and Carrie encourage Miranda that her new guy is definitely interested in her even though he didn't ask her out for a second date. But Berger sits in silence until Miranda suddenly asks for *his* opinion. With the door open wide to share his thoughts, Berger sets Miranda and the other women straight on the ways of men.

After this episode aired, the now infamous catchphrase "he's just not that into you" could be overheard at cubicles, boutiques, and brunch tables across America. Like Miranda, women everywhere had their eyes opened. If a guy is into you, then there's no need to analyze his meaning, call him, text him, stalk him, second-guess his actions, or pursue him. If he's into you, you will know it. Gone are the common excuses women make for men: commitment phobia, fear of ruining the friendship, mother issues, busy at work (a.k.a. cheating)—now women know the truth: "he's just not that into you."

From this now legendary line a hold-no-punches best seller sprang that dissects the common excuses women give as to why their current love interest is waffling in his affections or attentions. The book is naturally titled *He's Just Not That into You*. The authors, Greg Behrendt and Liz Tuccilo, shoot straight with women as to how men operate. It's simple really. If the man is *into* you, he will do whatever it takes to let you know it. To say this phrase became part of our vernacular is an understatement. Even Oprah hosted an entire show on the subject. Blogs and chat rooms buzzed with the new catchphrase.

I've never been one who would settle for a simple answer or a cliché excuse. I want to know why. *Why* is a big thing with me. I love solving mysteries. Puzzles intrigue me. I want to know the why, the reason, and the story behind the story.

My detective-like personality was in full effect when the best-selling book *He's Just Not That into You* hit the shelves and rocked single-girl world. I was intrigued, or should I say perplexed, by the immense popularity of this chick read. I wasn't perplexed because the writing isn't good. More so, I was curious

> Sex doesn't make you special; it just makes you available.

to know *why* women were buying this book in droves. What was the underlying pull behind this best seller? Why did this phrase raise such a fuss? Let's dig into this powerful little phrase and find out, shall we?

Personally, I think there is some good advice in the book, although I wouldn't endorse all of the content. For instance, the authors say, "If a guy isn't having sex with you, he's just not that into you."[6] I totally disagree! Sure, a guy will be physically attracted to a woman that he is into. But a true indicator of how into you a guy really is, is if he is willing to wait for you. *If a man is into you, he will treat you like a treasure.* If I can be frank, and by now you know I can, let me just say, a guy can hook up with anyone. Sex doesn't make you special; it just makes you available. Real men tell me all the time that the more they like a girl, and the more they see long-term potential with her, the more they want to wait for her and treat her like a treasure. Despite what the book might say, men who are into you will wait for you.

Back to the book: on a positive note, the authors do speak some much-needed truth to women. For example, Greg says, "Men, for the most part, like to pursue women. We like not knowing if we can catch you. We feel rewarded when we do."[7] Hats off to Greg on that one. I appreciate his candor because I long for the day when women stop chasing men and wise up to the fact that men by nature are hunters and love a good challenge. It's a personal pet peeve of mine to watch my generation of women chase men. For some reason our generation believes that being the aggressor in a relationship is the way to win a man's heart. Today, girls call, text, e-mail, instant message, ask out, and flat-out pursue. While I'm not an advocate of game playing, I do recognize the truth that is wired into men's God-given design: they love the chase. When women become the pursuer, it ultimately backfires.

Reflecting on the enormous impact that this line has had on women, I stop and ask myself two questions.

> I long for the day when women stop chasing men and wise up to the fact that men by nature are hunters and love a good challenge.

First, what will women talk about now that we don't need to analyze men anymore? Seriously ladies, our cell phone bills could reach an all-time low now that we no longer need to ask the age-old question, "Do you really think he likes me?" You know you do it. We all do. Here's a classic scenario: You just happen to run into a cute guy at work. The two of you have a brief encounter about the CSI episode from the night before, and then you spend two hours e-mailing and texting your girlfriends in order to decipher what happened in your two-minute chat. Was he flirting? Is he going to call? Do you think "see ya" literally meant "I'll see you soon," or was it only his way of saying "good-bye"?

I love being a girl; we are so pathetically funny.

The second and most important question I ask myself concerning *He's Just Not That into You* is: *Why* is a book like this even necessary? *Why* is it we need a *guy* to say, "Honey . . . wake up! Know your worth as a woman. Any man who is worthy of you will pursue you." *Why* is it we need an advice book on dating to tell us that we really are worth fighting for? *Why* is it we need a guy to point out that, frankly, women have become a little desperate?

Could it be that we are a generation of women who don't know we are worth the chase?

The primary message of the book *He's Just Not That into You* is that women do not realize their true value.

But my problem with the book is that the authors never tell women how to solve the problem—how a woman can know her real value. Greg admitted in his closing remarks that he can diagnose the problem, but it is up to each woman to change how she sees herself. This is where we need help. How does a woman know at the core of her being that she is a treasure, that she is loved, adored, and, yes, worth the chase? The authors did a fine job of diagnosing the problem, but they really didn't offer a solution. Simply telling a woman that she is worth more isn't enough. Something foundational must shift in a woman's heart and mind in order for her to truly believe she is a treasure.

> *We desperately want someone to tell us our worth and identity, but we are looking in the wrong place; therefore, we never find what we are looking for.*

In my detective work on this issue, I've come to see a connection between my generation's lack of worth and the lifestyle endorsed on *Sex and the City*. It seems to me that one is feeding the other. The more we go "looking for love in all the wrong places," the more we end up feeling empty, ashamed, and devalued. There is a vicious cycle that results from the *Sex and the City* lifestyle. When a woman goes looking for the love her soul craves in any source other than God Himself, she finds herself more confused than ever about her real worth as a woman.

- Am I lovable only *if* I'm considered beautiful?
- Is my value as a woman *really* found in being desired by a man?
- Am I accepted only *when* someone else approves of me?

Over and over again, women give themselves away at the altars of approval, sex, relationships, food, and fashion. We turn to these substitutes in hopes of finding and receiving the unconditional love our souls are searching for. But in reality, we walk away empty.

- Robbed of our true identity.
- Stripped of our true worth.
- Separated from our true love.
- We still haven't found what we are looking for.

Outside of the real love that our hearts crave, we simply don't know who we are. Which brings us back to where we first began. We are women who really long to be rescued. Instead of knowing we are loved and believing we are worth the chase, women are clamoring, grasping, clinging, needing, and hoping someone will tell us we are wanted, loved, and adored. It is so very exhausting.

We desperately want to feel loved. We desperately want someone to tell us our worth and identity, but we are looking in the wrong place; therefore, we never find what we are looking for. Over and over again in this pursuit, we hear the same message that says, "He's just not that into you," and we take those words on as our identity. We walk away thinking, *I'm not worth it. I'm not lovable. I wasn't chosen.* Ironically, the primary message of a different best-selling book is: HE *is* just that into *you.* And, girlfriends, that book is the Bible. And yes, the "He" is God Himself.

The Bible is the first action-adventure love story, and God stars as the ultimate hero. It is the story of God's rescue mission to redeem His Beloved, you and me, from the perpetual emptiness and insecurity that resulted from our separation from Him. Women's hearts swoon at the thought of the knight in shining armor rushing in to save the day, and that is exactly what God did for each one of us when He stepped out of the magnificence of heaven and became a man in Jesus Christ. Think about it: the God who *invented* night brings out His shining armor for us.

In the very beginning, when humanity was first separated from God because of sin, God promised that He would make all things right again. God said that One would come who would destroy Satan and *rescue* God's people. Remember Charlotte's longing to be rescued? Her desire is rooted in this promise.

Nothing in us is inherently *deserving of* this rescue

because we, too, like Adam and Eve, chose rebellion against God. It's plain and simple: we got ourselves into this mess. But God delights in getting us out. That's the amazing part of the whole story. Don't miss it! God proves how awe-inspiring and incredible He is by rescuing us even when we aren't deserving of it. His original promise to rescue us was fulfilled when God became a man in Jesus Christ and died a sacrificial death in our place. The death of God sounds absurd to many, but Jesus had to die in order to restore the relationship we were designed to have with our Creator. As it says in the Bible, "Jesus Christ rescued us from this evil world we're in by offering himself as a sacrifice for our sins. God's plan is that we all experience that rescue" (Gal. 1:4 MSG).

What girl doesn't love the grand gestures? We want love expressed to us in a way that is loud, clear, and dramatic—like in the final episode of *Sex and the City* when Mr. Big jumps on an airplane and flies to Paris in order to find Carrie and confess his true love to her. Some guys *say* it and then some guys *prove* their love with actions. God does both. While God is a God of words, He is also one of extravagant gestures. God expressed His love for us in the most dramatic fashion when He experienced pain and suffering so that you and I could experience love and peace. Yes, Jesus faced death so that you and I could have life. His love is bold, extravagant, sacrificial, and grand.

Grasping the depths of God's love for me absolutely transformed my life. I'm just a girl who spent a lifetime looking for love and living with intense insecurity because I had no clue that it could be different. I didn't realize a life of real satisfaction and real security was even an option. I thought I would always need alcohol to boost my confidence and would live dependent on a guy's attention and affection to make me feel loved. When I understood the meaning and the implications of God's rescue mission, it rocked my world. The reason *why* this truth transformed me is that finally, I felt loved. And in this love, I finally found my worth, my value, and my true identity.

Value

As I write this final chapter, I am in New Orleans, Louisiana. I'm not here for Mardi Gras, nor am I here for the Super Bowl or any of the other major party events that draw crowds to this city by the thousands. No, I'm in the Crescent City for something much more low-key: an antiques auction.

My friend and I hopped in the car and drove six hours to New Orleans after work this weekend. Road trip essentials loaded: her dog, my laptop, cookies, bottles of water, two grande vanilla lattes, and tons of girl talk to keep us occupied at least until the state line. After a couple of detours (a special thank-you to the waiter at Cracker Barrel for the Coca-Cola cake and for allowing me to charge up my computer) and one scary gas station experience, we finally arrived at the auction.

I was there purely as an observer; my friend is the one with an eye for fine things. I'm always blown away by her ability to see something that I would totally overlook and to proceed to tell me the hundred-plus creative ways the said item could be used, displayed, and adorned. She's just got the knack.

Auction people are really funny. I'm a little bit of an obsessive people watcher to begin with, so put me in a room with a hundred people with money to spend and three-hundred-year-old antiques on the line and I am oh-so-entertained! They are all very serious, you know. For weeks prior to the auction the attendees perused the catalog that displayed the items for sale: paintings, porcelain, china, armoires, rugs, chairs, beds, and something called a commode, which wasn't at all what I thought it would be. (I'm so high class it hurts.) And then the auction began.

You could tell immediately that there were a few items high on everyone's list. And then, there were the duds. Some pieces evoked fun bidding wars as the auctioneer and attendees swiveled their necks back and forth to see the opposing paddles rise and fall with the call of a price. I would have instigated one or two just for fun, but the prices exceeded my limit of fifteen dollars by a couple of zeros and I feared actually winning the bid. So I settled back in my seat for a day of observation. And do you want to know what I discovered at the auction? I learned this incredible truth: an item is worth what someone is willing to pay for it.

An item is worth what someone is willing to pay for it.

I came to this conclusion during one of the more intense bidding wars of the day. The antique wasn't that special to me. But then again, what do I know? But as soon as the lot number was announced, the atmosphere in the room cranked up a notch. With bidders on the phone and at least three in the room, the battle to win the eighteenth-century American armoire began. Higher and higher the dollar amount grew as eager and able buyers raised their hands to bid on the piece. The piece was expected to go for a much lower amount, but in an auction, the buyer determines the value. To me it was just an old armoire, but to the person doing the bidding, it was a treasure. And in the end, the value determined by the buyer was outrageous.

What does an antiques auction have to do with you and me? This experience taught me a great deal about the value of a person. You are worth and I am worth what someone is willing to pay for us. The incredible truth is that God paid for you and for me with the life of His Son. He *is just that into you*. The Bible says,

> *For you know that God paid a ransom to save*
> *you from the empty life you inherited from your*
> *ancestors. And the ransom he paid was not mere*
> *gold or silver. It was the precious blood of Christ,*
> *the sinless, spotless Lamb of God. God chose him*
> *as your ransom long before the world began, but*
> *he has now revealed him to you in these last days.*
> *1 Peter 1:18–20 NLT*

Our lives were purchased with something more precious than gold or silver. When God decided to purchase our lives, He paid the highest price that could be paid—the life of His Son, Jesus.

We've been talking about looking for love in all the wrong places, yet the big question that remains is, how do we stop looking? We can call off the dogs and stop searching for love when we find it. Here's the amazing thing: you and I don't need to search for love because *Love* came looking for us. Love's name is Jesus. If you want to know what you are worth, the only one who is able to tell you is God, and He says you are worth dying for. . . . Stop. Think about this truth for a minute. God says you are worth dying for.

We can't even comprehend the love that propelled that kind of sacrifice.

Why does all this really matter? At the end of the day does it matter one iota that Jesus died for me? Absolutely it matters, because the love of God is what tells you who you are and what fills your soul. How do you see yourself? I've asked this question several times in the course of this book. Are you a treasure? Are you lovable? Are you a mistake? I've come to realize it doesn't matter how beautiful, successful, or talented a woman is; if she doesn't know *who* she is, those things are never enough. What's my point? This whole business of "looking for love in all the wrong places" is really just about a woman's heart desiring to know one thing—*am I loved?* This emptiness and insecurity are the life we all long to be rescued from, and the separation that caused it is exactly why Jesus paid with His own life to rescue us. The question that remains is, how will you respond to God's grand gesture of love?

Freed to Love

I heard a story one time about Abraham Lincoln. Legend has it that he attended a slave auction (ironically, in New Orleans) years before he became president of the United States. Lincoln watched from a distance as one by one men and women were brought before the crowd to be auctioned to the highest bidder.

After watching in disgust for a while, he turned to go when he saw a young woman brought to the platform to be sold. Her eyes gleamed with anger, and her chin jutted out with defiance.

Her asking price would be high because she was perfect for work on a plantation. The auctioneer started the bidding and many hands went up. One hand in particular was that of Abraham Lincoln himself. And he kept raising his hand that day until he bought her.

Once the deal was done and she belonged to him, Lincoln walked up to her and said the unthinkable: "You are free." Her face bore the same look of anger and defiance that she wore as her worth had been determined on that platform. Glaring at him she spat out, "Free for what?" Lincoln said, "You are free. Free to go. I bought you in order to set you free." As the truth settled into her heart, the expression upon her face softened and with love overflowing, she said, "Then I'm going with *you*." Any of us out there who have been enslaved to the bad habits of looking for love in all the wrong places will pause here, *feeling* the parallel of what Christ did for us—He paid a high price for us to set us free. And if we choose to accept that freedom, then we will come to the same conclusion as that young woman: the safest place for us is with HIM.

Girlfriends, as a woman who made the choice to "go with Jesus," I am here to tell you that the love, security, identity, and comfort we search for is found in Him.

The Offer

I try to imagine myself as the fifth wheel in the *Sex and the City* crew. Would they listen to me if I shared the wonderful story of the God who loves each one of them so much He left everything in order to rescue them? Would they believe that Jesus is just that into them? Or would they tilt their heads and stare at me as if I'd lost my mind?

I picture Charlotte and her idealistic hopes and dreams—always looking for Mr. Right—and I wonder, *Would she believe me if I told her He's been pursuing her for years?* What about Miranda? Is she so determined to be self-sufficient and independent that she'd never admit that she needs to be rescued? What about Carrie? Would our favorite fashion queen believe there is a love that can define her that doesn't involve a man or require a new pair of Choos? Last but not least, Samantha. I bet you thought I forgot her. I didn't. I just can't quote her most of the time. So what about Sam? Would she believe God's love could include a girl like her? And what about you? Do you believe God's love includes a girl like you?

The amazing thing about this God story is that He came to rescue girls from every walk of life. The starry-eyed Charlotte, the serious Miranda, the care-free Carrie, and yes, even the shocking Samantha—each woman is precious to Jesus Christ. So it doesn't matter which of these characters you identify with the most—or if they are all foreign to you—the God of the Universe finds you worth dying for. He moved heaven and earth in order to rescue you and give you the love you've been looking for.

Girls, HE IS JUST THAT INTO YOU!

Appendix

Dear Friend,

Perhaps after reading *Sex and the City Uncovered* you've realized you need to be rescued. You are emotionally and spiritually exhausted from "looking for love in all the wrong places," and you know your soul is crying out for God.

Below is a sample prayer—it is only a guideline. Prayer is simply having a conversation with God. All you need to do is express your heart to Him. The main thing is that you agree with God that you are a sinner and you need Jesus to come to your rescue.

"Rescue Me" Prayer

Father God,

I need help. I know I need to be rescued!

I realize I was created by You and for a relationship with You, and apart from You I am empty, searching, and without true peace. I confess that I am a sinner and I willfully chose to rebel against You. I believe that Jesus Christ is Your Son and that He came to earth to rescue humanity from the prison and consequences of sin. I acknowledge and turn away from my sin [list everything that comes to mind], and I claim the forgiveness and grace offered to me through the sacrificial death of Jesus Christ. I believe by faith that Jesus died for me on the cross and He rose again from the grave. I believe He is alive today that I might have new life in Him. By faith I receive this gift.

I give You my life.

Take all of me.

Thank You, Jesus, for coming to my rescue.

In the name of Christ I pray,

Amen

If you prayed this prayer, or if you've expressed something similar in the past, I bet you're asking, "Now what? Where do I go from here?" In this book I chronicled the various ways we in vain attempt to fill the God-spot in our souls. I've also uncovered the many pitfalls associated with these empty pursuits. So, what do we do now? From one woman who was looking for love to another, I'd like to give you a few words of advice that changed my life:

1. **Fall in love with Jesus**. I realized early on that I would never live for God if my heart didn't love Him. As long as I loved happy hour or the next hot guy more than Jesus, then my faith wasn't going very far. Examine your heart; if you don't love Him, simply ask God to change your heart. The best prayer I've ever prayed is "Jesus, please give me a heart to love You more than anything else in this world." Girlfriends, just let me say that God loves to answer this one. Today I am so in love with Jesus that I have butterflies! He is my one true and holy passion.

2. **Pray for and seek out girlfriends who love God**. The second best prayer I ever prayed is for girlfriends who love Jesus and desire to live their lives for Him. I'm here to testify to the fact that God answers this prayer too! I am continually blown away by how God has provided me with the most amazing friends. Here's the thing about your girlfriends: we tend to become like the people we spend time hanging out with. If the crowd you hang with is pursuing emptiness, then it will be hard for you to pursue things of real value. Carefully consider whom you want to be like. Each of my closest friends possesses character qualities that I admire and long to emulate. They also encourage me, love me, speak truth

to me, and hold me accountable. My girlfriends live for God, and I know without them in my life today that I would still be looking for love in all the empty places I described in this book.

3. ***Get in God's Word!*** Studying the Bible transformed my life. Let me suggest that you begin today reading the Bible. Start with the Gospel of John and simply ask God to teach you more about Jesus. Next, find a church that teaches the Bible and dive in. Not only does God use the Bible to speak to us today, but God's Word also says our lives are transformed by simply absorbing God's truth. As you read the Word, you will begin to see yourself and this world as God sees it. As a result, the insecurity, emptiness, and unrest you feel in your heart will begin to fade away as your mind is filled with the power of God's truth. You will know your true worth as a woman, and you will begin to feel and experience God's amazing love for you.

4. ***Get involved in a local church.*** Here's a fact that most people don't realize: we are hardwired to worship God. Worship is our human response to who God is. We have this inner drive to express back to God praise for His greatness and goodness. Find a local church and make regu-

lar attendance to Bible study and worship a priority in your life. Here's the benefit: not only will worship feed your soul, but you will also be blessed by the fellowship of other Christians. God designed us to be in community. We can't fly solo! The church is God's plan for this world until Jesus Christ returns. Find a church that teaches the Bible and begin using your gifts and talents to serve God alongside other followers of Jesus Christ.

Recommended Resources

The Search for Significance: Seeing Your True Worth through God's Eyes by Robert McGee (W Publishing Group, 2003).

The 10 Commandments of Dating: Time-Tested Laws for Building Successful Relationships by Ben Young and Dr. Samuel Adams (Nelson Reference, 1999).

I Am Not but I Know I AM: Welcome to the Story of God by Louie Giglio (Multnomah, 2005).

Waking the Dead: The Glory of a Heart Fully Alive by John Eldredge (Nelson Books, 2003).

Breaking Free: Making Liberty in Christ a Reality in Life by Beth Moore (B & H Publishing Group, 2000).

Jesus, the One and Only by Beth Moore (B & H Publishing Group, 2002).

The Purpose Driven Life: What on Earth Am I Here For? by Rick Warren (Zondervan, 2007).

Your Single Treasure: Good News about Singles and Sexuality by Rick Stedman (Moody Publishers, 2000).

Kissed the Girls and Made Them Cry: Why We Lose When We Give In by Lisa Bevere (Nelson Books, 2002).

Discussion Questions

Chapter One: The Sex and the City Life

1. What elements of Marian's story do you connect with?

2. All of us go through life with some insecurities. Identify some of your own insecurities and methods you use to mask them.

3. Define the "modern single girl" as seen in various modes of the entertainment industry.

4. How does the world tell us we should try and fill "our empty glass"?

5. Introspectively, can you identify a decision that led to a chain of events that directed the course of your life for a time? Would you modify that decision based on what you know now?

6. "There is a God-shaped vacuum in the heart of every man which cannot be filled by any created thing, but only by God Himself" (Pascal). Do you agree with Pascal's thesis regarding our emptiness? Why or why not?

Chapter Two: Looking for Love in All the Wrong Places

1. Which *Sex and the City* character, as described in this chapter, do you identify with the most? Why?

2. "Women just really want to be rescued." Agree/Disagree

3. Describe how you/we "look for love in all the wrong places."

4. Have you ever felt "captive to emptiness"? How does emptiness create a prison in our lives?

5. What lies are we as females told by the world from the time we are small through maturity? Who tells us these lies?

6. Compare and contrast Adam and Eve's life in the garden before and after the apple. What did they gain? What did they lose? Was eating the apple worth it?

Chapter Three: Looking for Love in Mr. Right

1. We are all in a constant state of looking for the perfect guy, the perfect shoe, the perfect black dress, and the perfect hairstyle—all seem elusive. Talk about your current "searches" or "thirsts."

2. What thirst did the woman at the well have that she hadn't recognized?

3. Jesus offers the woman at the well/us a different kind of water: "But whoever drinks from the water

that I will give him will never get thirsty again—ever!" (John 4:13). Discuss the implications of Jesus's meeting our thirsts.

4. Define *God-spot*, according to the text.

5. How are acceptance and security related to unconditional love?

Chapter Four: Looking for Love in Approval

1. Where do you/we look for approval?

2. Describe some labels that you have had to live with since junior high. Where did those labels come from? Are you still living with them, or have you rejected the labels of the past?

3. Do you believe that the appearance factor and the performance factor are strong motivators in the daily decisions we make? How? Why?

4. What defines you?

5. Rejection and acceptance both have an impact on the way we view ourselves. Journal or discuss an example of each from the recent past. How did you handle the rejection? The acceptance?

6. Jesus gave the sinful woman at the party a new label: "_____" (Luke 7:40–50), after she had been rejected by all the townspeople. You/we are not rejected by Christ in our present state; we are accepted, forgiven, and loved. What kind of effect do you think Jesus's acceptance had on the sinful woman's life?

Chapter Five: Looking for Love in a Hook-up

1. Identify what (or whom) you are still looking for.

2. Is there such a thing as "sex without strings"? Agree/disagree. What strings come with being sexually active?

3. Do you know someone who reminds you of the woman the temple leaders wanted to stone? How is she treated by the world? In what radical way did Jesus respond to her?

4. Identify a time when you felt condemned by your friends due to your actions. Discuss the impact of the condemnation.

5. Has anyone ever just loved you right where you were, no matter what you had done wrong? Compare and contrast the condemnation of the world with the way Jesus loved the woman accused of adultery.

6. How does God's promise of "beauty for ashes" apply to you/us?

7. Relate "What looks like rejection is God's protection" with hindsight to a painful rejection.

8. How is God's design for sex for our own good?

Chapter Six: Looking for Love at Happy Hour

1. Explain what C. S. Lewis meant when he said, "What does not satisfy when we find it was not the thing we were desiring."

2. Describe and detail your "happy hour" elements. Or fill in the blank: "comfort _____ is my comfort zone."

3. Are you currently "running on empty"? Reflect on a time when your red light was flashing. Who or what is/was siphoning your gas? Propose a possible solution to this dilemma.

4. Proverbs 14:12 says, "There is a way that seems right to a man, but its end is the way to death." What type of death is Proverbs referring to? How does this apply to us?

5. In John 10:10 Jesus said, "A thief comes only to steal and to kill and to destroy. I have come that they may have life and have it in abundance." What has been stolen, killed, or destroyed in your life? Define an abundant life in your own words. Discuss the contrast.

6. Examining the parallel of the Vine and the branch with our lives relying on Jesus, how can we stay connected and dependent on the Vine of Jesus today?

Chapter Seven: He *Is* Just That into You!

1. Describe something or someone you view as a treasure. What makes that thing or person valuable? Do you believe God views you as a treasure?

2. What do you believe must shift in values and perceptions in this present-day culture for people to view themselves and others as a "treasure"?

3. Compose a list of five characteristics you view as valuable about yourself. How would you classify those characteristics: intrinsic or extrinsic?

4. Who or what do you believe develops intrinsic characteristics?

5. Identify a time when you felt empty. Examine who or what created that emptiness. Describe how that affected your view of yourself and others around you.

6. If you were asked, "What are you worth?" how would you respond? On what are you basing your response?

7. "An item is worth what someone is willing to pay for it" (p. 172). Agree or disagree? Why?

8. According to 1 Peter 1:18–20, what grand gesture did God make in order to rescue us (p. 173)?

9. Connect God's gesture to what you/we are worth in His eyes.

Acknowledgments

S *ex and the City Uncovered* is without a doubt the result of the Body of Christ at work. When I say I could never have written this book on my own, I mean every word. The writing process was a collaborative effort of so many who contributed their gifts and talents because they shared one vision: to reach women with the life-changing love of Jesus Christ.

To Catherine King and Angel Texada (your names should be on the cover), thank you for the hours you invested editing and for challenging me to become a better writer. Catherine, praise God for your eye for detail. Angel, thank you for helping me find my funny.

To Toni Richmond, Jeremy Good, and Anita Pahor for your gift of encouragement; I would never have written the first word had you not "challenged" (pestered, hassled, and prodded) me to follow God's call on my life.

Brad Goad, thank you for listening to the Lord and mailing the manuscript!

I could never have written this book without my accountability group Leti Lusk, Susannah Baker, and Leigh Kohler, as well as my mentor Tonya Riggle (aka FEMA). One word describes you—strength. You stood by me through the intense pain and the unbelievable joy of this process and I am forever blessed by your love and friendship.

To the "think tank:" you answered my questions and endured my crazy ideas for months. (Megan Thomas, Amy Sandidge, Kim Foxxen, Shannon Burkett, Kim Wilhite, Joy Willoughby, Sara Fuselier, Veronica Villarreal, Holly Gilbert, and Jennifer Abbott) Thank you for sharing your amazing insights.

The true miracle workers in this process are the prayer warriors. You are the reason this book is a reality. Mom and Dad, Jeff and Jenny Venghaus, Matt and Jessica Trozzo, Clint and Amy Sandidge, Dave and Tonya Riggle, Ben and Elliott Young, Lacey and Chris Dahse, Becky Henson, Lauren Hall, Muriel Pope, Manonne Johnson, Megan Thomas, Meredith Perryman, Christy Wilhite, Kimberley Roth, Talitha Bullock, Reagan Van Steenis, Jeannene Simonton, Dr. Jim DeLoach, Steve Seelig, Pam Thompson, Pam Mitchell, the 2007 and 2008 classes of Second Baptist School and the FUEL Bible Study.) I felt your prayers and will always remember how God provided and proved He does indeed "move the mountains."

Special thanks go to my home church, Second Baptist Church of Houston, Texas. To Dr. Ed Young and Ben Young—thank you for preaching the Word of God—I am a life that was changed. To the SingleLife Ministry (Lisa Milne, Liz Crystal, and Chris Dahse), thank you for your ministry and for making *Sex and the City . . . The Rest of the Story* a reality.

I also want to thank my new friends at B & H Publishing Group: To Ken Stephens and David Shepherd for giving this girl a chance and to Tom Walters for your patience with me as a new author. To all the wonderful people in the editorial, marketing, and sales departments—your support has been priceless.

Finally, to my Mom and Dad, thank you for your prayers, support, and always modeling the walk of faith.

About the Author

Have you ever seen a street after a parade? The lonesome scraps and fragments that are left seem dirty, abandoned, and trashed. Run over. What a shift from the moment before when music trilled, drums beat, people danced, and colors burst through our senses, drawing us closer and closer, the goal to press as closely to the barricade as humanly possible. What fun! What exhilaration! What glitter! What a draw! And then . . . it's gone. Passed. Done. Confetti becomes litter, songs trail to silence, and the attraction of the crowd dwindles and dies. This is how Marian Jordan describes her life without Jesus Christ.

Fun, loud, colorful, cyclical . . . lonely and trashed.

Her sharp observation of the party years resonate with the familiar. Her transparent account of the lure of fashion, sex, booze, and approval chronicle the dilemma of the "every girl" in today's society.

Marian's powerful testimony of coming to brokenness and emptiness and her dynamic account of the gentle mercy and forceful grace of Christ, who called her into His arms, permeate all of her writings and speaking engagements. Whole in Christ and ready to tell any ear that will listen, Marian has a passion for young women who flock to the parade of emptiness.

She is a dynamic speaker that leaves indelible marks on her audience: painful rib cages from laughter and mind-searing impressions of being so-dead-on to one's private dilemmas. Marian has the gift of applying sound biblical truth to the tender wounds of bleeding hearts. The girl can teach. The girl can relate. And the girl can move a wounded heart to change, through an introduction to Jesus Christ, the Lord and Lover of her soul.

Today Marian is the founder of Redeemed Girl Ministries. She is an active speaker, guest lecturer, and published author. She lives in Houston where she is finishing her master's degree at Southwestern Seminary and serves at her home church, Second Baptist Church of Houston, when not on the road at speaking engagements. Though she is a Texas girl at heart, she feels at home in destinations all over the world: Australia, Costa Rica, Italy, England, Lufkin, New York, Magnolia. She finds God's beauty in every country, city, and small town that she happens upon. So now, when she does come across a parade, she can soak in the excitement and walk away content, knowing that the Master of Ceremonies will go with her to the next town, the next country, the next season of life. And that, friends, is the beauty of being a Redeemed Girl.

If you are interested in Marian Jordan speaking at your conference or event, contact www.marianjordan.com and www.redeemedgirl.com.

Redeemed Girl Ministries
12335 Kingsride #239
Houston, Texas 77024-4116

Notes

1. Janice Shaw Crouse, *Love Potion Number "O,"* Concerned Women for America, www.beverlylahayein stitute.org/articledisplay.asp?id=9936 (Jan. 19, 2006).

2. Ibid.

3. Grace Alexandra, "Emotional Bonding," *Xt3* Christian magazine, www.xt3.com/magazine/article .asp?id=141 (2004).

4. The statistics are from "Safe Sex and the Facts" by Raymond G. Bohlin, Ph.D., from his article at www. leadru.com.

5. Joe S. McIlhaney Jr., M.D., *Sex, What You Don't Know Can Kill You* (Grand Rapids: Baker Books), 19, 23, 30, 42, 57, 59, 63, 95.

6. Greg Behrendt and Liz Tuccilo, *He's Just Not That into You* (Simon Spotlight Entertainment, 2006), 47.

7. Ibid., 16.